W9-BRE-439

CHILDCRAFT

THE HOW AND WHY LIBRARY

ART AROUND US

World Book, Inc.
a Scott Fetzer company
Chicago

Childcraft—The How and Why Library
(Reg. U.S. Pat. and T.M. Off.—Marca Registrada)

World Book, Inc.
233 N. Michigan Avenue
Chicago, IL 60601

Childcraft—The How and Why Library ISBN 0-7166-0197-4
Art Around Us ISBN 0-7166-0152-4
Library of Congress Catalog Card Number 98-75114
Printed in the United States of America
1 2 3 4 5 6 7 8 9 06 05 04 03 02 01 00

Contents

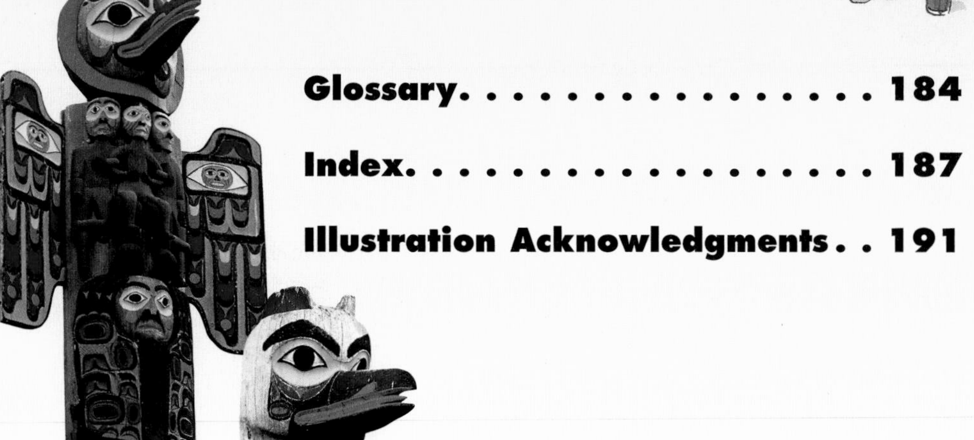

Introduction

What is art? When someone asks you that question, you might think of a beautiful painting hanging on the wall in a museum. Or you might remember a statue you saw in the park. Maybe you think of something you made out of colored paper or clay in art class. All these things are art. Crafts, paintings, and sculptures that people make for others to look at are called visual arts. But they are not the only kinds of art. When you sing or play an instrument to create music, that is also art. So is the puppet show you put on for your parents, and so is the play at the theater. These kinds of art are called performing arts.

So art is something people make or do for others to enjoy. It is art because it gets people to use their imagination, both to create it and to enjoy it.

This book, *Art Around Us,* explores the visual arts of crafts, painting, and sculpture. You will learn how these arts developed in various parts of the world, and you will find out what materials and ideas are used to create works of art. The book also explores the performing arts of music and theater. It describes different kinds of performances around the world, and you'll discover how to make music and put on a play.

There are many features in this book to help you find your way through it. You'll find fun-filled facts and extra information inside the boxes marked **Know It All!** You can amaze your friends with what you learn!

The book also has many activities that you can do at home. Look for the words **Try This!** over a colored ball. The activity that follows offers a way to learn more about art. For example, you can cut out a paper lantern, make your own paint, or form clay into shapes.

Know It All! boxes have fun-filled facts.

Each activity has a number. The higher the number, the more adult help you may need.

An activity that has this colorful border is a little more complex than one without the border.

Each activity has a number in its colored ball. Activities with a 1 in a green ball are simplest to do. Those with a 2 in a yellow ball may require a little adult help with tasks such as cutting or measuring. Activities with a 3 in a red ball may need more adult help.

A Try This! activity that has a colorful border around its entire page is a little more complex or requires a few more materials. Take a moment to review the list of materials needed and to read the step-by-step instructions before you begin.

As you read this book, you will see that some words are printed in bold type, **like this.** These are words that might be new to you. You can find the meanings and pronunciations of these words in the **Glossary**. Turn to the **Index** to look up page numbers of subjects that interest you the most.

If you enjoy learning about art, find out more about it in other resources. Here are just a few. Check them out at a bookstore or at your local or school library.

- **Barry's Scrapbook: A Window into Art,** Video, American Library Association, 1994, 42 minutes. *Have fun and learn, too, as you look at art, learn about art, sing about art, and create art with Barry.*
- **A Caldecott Celebration,** by Leonard S. Marcus, 1998. *Six Caldecott Medal artists share their life stories.*
- **A Child's Book of Play in Art,** selected by Lucy Micklethwait, 1996. *In looking at great works of art, children can learn vocabulary, patterning, feelings, play, and much more.*
- **Crafts for Kids Who Are Wild about Dinosaurs,** by Kathy Ross, 1997. *This book contains 20 dinosaur-related projects that you can make from materials you have around the house.*
- **I Spy a Lion: Animals in Art,** devised and selected by Lucy Micklethwait, 1994. *Well known works of art become the focus for this "I spy" type of book.*
- **Let's Dance,** by George Ancona, 1998. *Illustrated with lively photographs, this book shares the joy of dance from many countries.*
- **Masks,** by Meryl Doney, 1995. *With easy-to-follow instructions, you can make masks from around the world.*
- **Meet the Orchestra,** by Ann Hayes, 1991. *A picture book with animals playing the instruments of the orchestra.*
- **Mouse Paint,** by Ellen Stoll Walsh, 1989. *A delightful picture book about mixing colors.*
- **The Rain or Shine Activity Book: Fun Things to Make and Do,** by Joanna Cole and Stephanie Calmenson, 1997. *From paper crafts to magic tricks, this book is filled with activities you will enjoy.*
- **Show-Me-How I Can Make Music,** by Michael Purton, 1996. *Young children will enjoy these simple-to-make musical instruments that are simple and fun to play.*

The Art of Crafts

Just look at the beautiful things people make with their hands. Paper folding, paper cutting, weaving, quilting, and pottery are all crafts. And there are many more.

Craftworkers make objects that people use in their daily life. The objects they make are often beautiful to look at and to touch because of the workers' skill. Each object is a work of art.

You can learn to be a craftworker, too. This chapter includes several useful things you can make. But before you begin each project, be sure to read all the directions and gather all the materials you will need. Then have fun completing the craft.

How Crafts Began

Most crafts are activities that have been done for a very long time. Some crafts developed in different parts of the world at the same time. For example, people in different parts of the world carved designs onto their wooden boats. Hundreds of years ago, a group of people called the Maori (MAH oh ree) were skilled woodcarvers as well as good sailors. They sailed from islands in northeast Polynesia to what is now New Zealand in canoes decorated with beautiful woodcarvings.

Thousands of miles away, in northern Europe, Viking sailors decorated the prow, or front, of their ships with woodcarvings called figureheads. The tradition of figureheads continued in Western Europe, North America, and South America as long as large wooden ships sailed the seas.

Other crafts were important in different places. One such craft is kitemaking. Almost two thousand years ago, Chinese generals used paper kites to signal their troops in battle.

Today, Japanese paint warriors on their kites and wage "war" in the air at kite festivals. They also celebrate Boys' Day on May 5 by flying kitelike windsocks. These paper flags are shaped and painted like carp—fish that stand for strength, courage, and determination in Japan.

Getting Crafty

To do all the crafts in this chapter, you will need lots of materials. Some things you will need for only one project. But other things you will use again and again.

It is a good idea to collect the materials listed on page 13 and keep them in a large cardboard box. Then you will have the materials you need to work with.

Where will you find your materials? You may have to buy some at a craft store. But you can start your collecting at home and outside. Remember to get permission before you add something to your collection. And be careful when handling sharp objects.

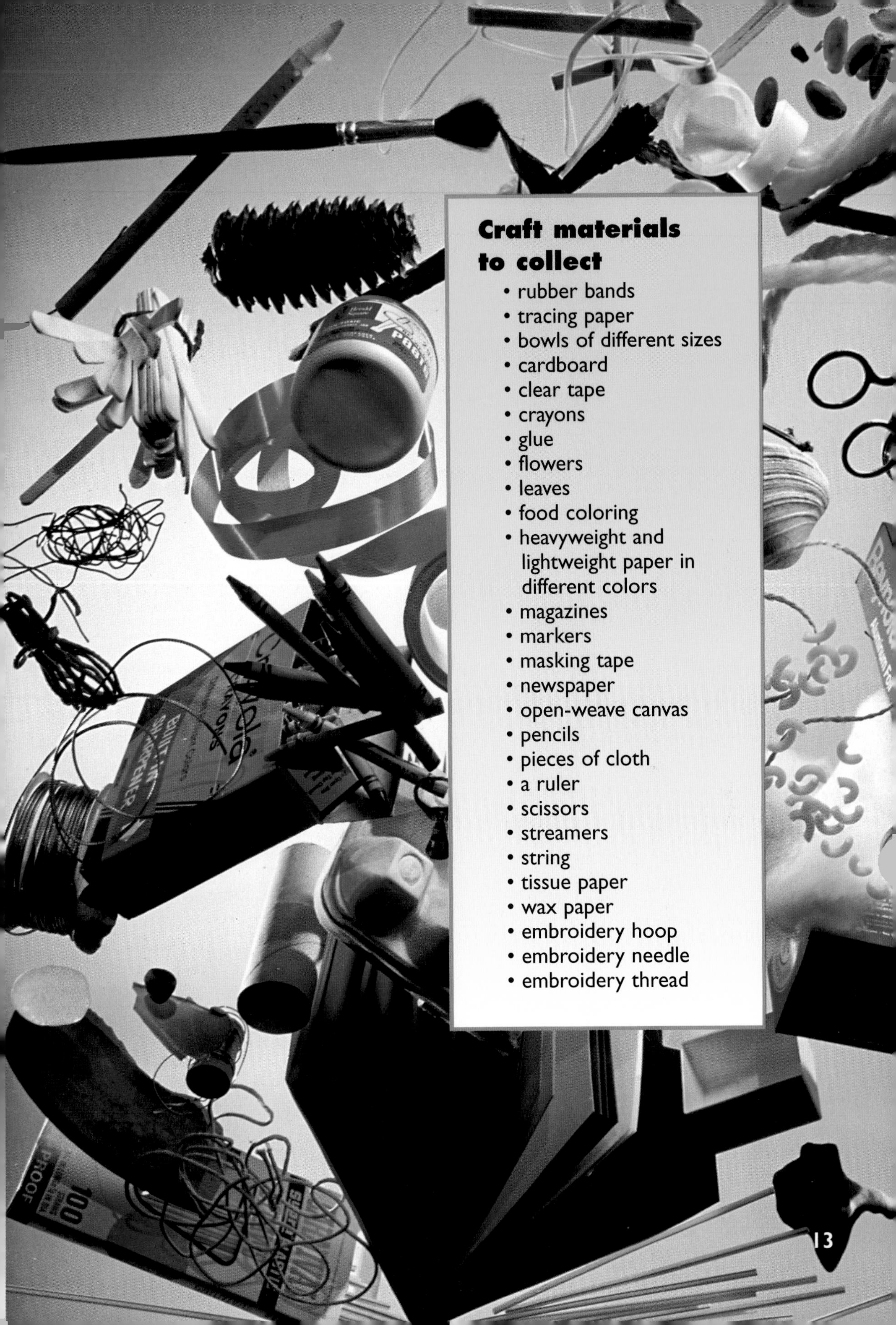

Craft materials to collect

- rubber bands
- tracing paper
- bowls of different sizes
- cardboard
- clear tape
- crayons
- glue
- flowers
- leaves
- food coloring
- heavyweight and lightweight paper in different colors
- magazines
- markers
- masking tape
- newspaper
- open-weave canvas
- pencils
- pieces of cloth
- a ruler
- scissors
- streamers
- string
- tissue paper
- wax paper
- embroidery hoop
- embroidery needle
- embroidery thread

Paper Folding

Have you ever made a paper airplane? If you have, you have enjoyed the most recent and popular addition to the old craft of paper folding. This craft is called ***origami*** (AWR uh GAH mee).

These origami figures are shaped like animals—a bird, a fish, a rooster, a bull, and an owl.

Originally, the Japanese invented about 100 origami figures. Most are natural forms, such as birds, frogs, and fish. One form of origami, with shapes all its own, is called *noshi.* These are pleated paper decorations that Japanese people attach to gifts.

The Japanese like to use squares of paper for origami. The squares range from 6 to 10 inches (15 to 25 centimeters) in size. They also use a special paper called *washi* (WAH shee).

KNOW It All!

The craft of paper folding began in China but became very popular in Japan. Even its name, *origami*, comes from Japanese words. *Ori* means "folding" and *gami* means "paper."

Papermaking families in Japan still make washi by hand. To make washi, they first mix a gluelike liquid with bark, cotton, linen, or tree fibers and stir the mixture into a mush called pulp.

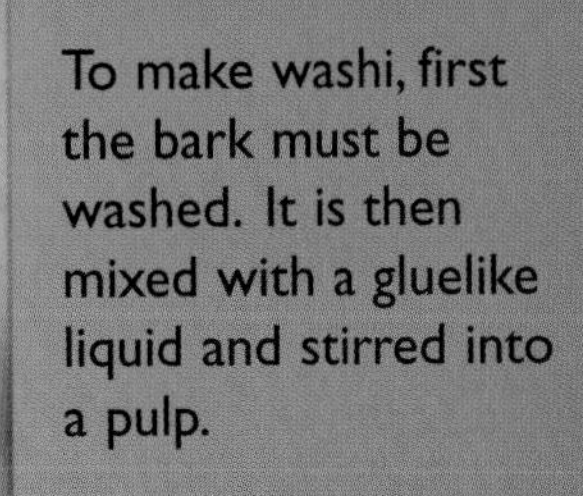

To make washi, first the bark must be washed. It is then mixed with a gluelike liquid and stirred into a pulp.

A special screen is dipped into the pulp.

Next, they dip a special screen into the pulp and drain out most of the moisture. Then, they place the wet sheets on flat surface to dry. The Japanese use the washi for umbrellas, kites, and origami.

The wet washi sheets are dried on a flat surface.

Fold It

Origami is enjoyed all around the world today. People in many countries have added new designs to the ones first created in Japan. Here are instructions for how to make paper dolls. Use them as puppets, decorations for packages, or write names on them and use them to assign seats for dinner.

You Will Need:

1 or more squares of light-colored paper

a pencil and marking pens

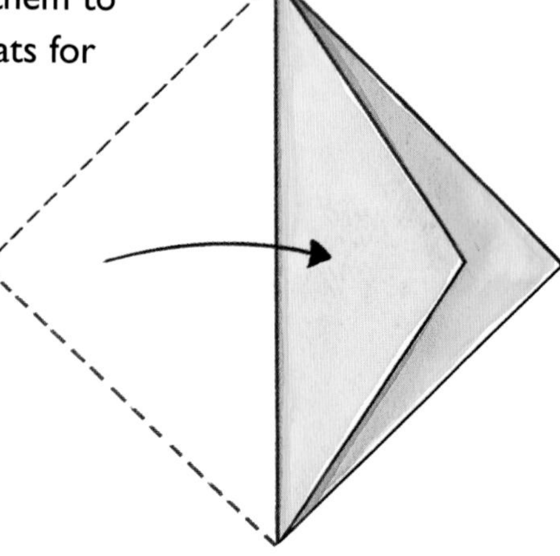

What To Do:

1. Fold a square of paper in half from corner to corner to make a crease that marks the center of the paper. Unfold the square.

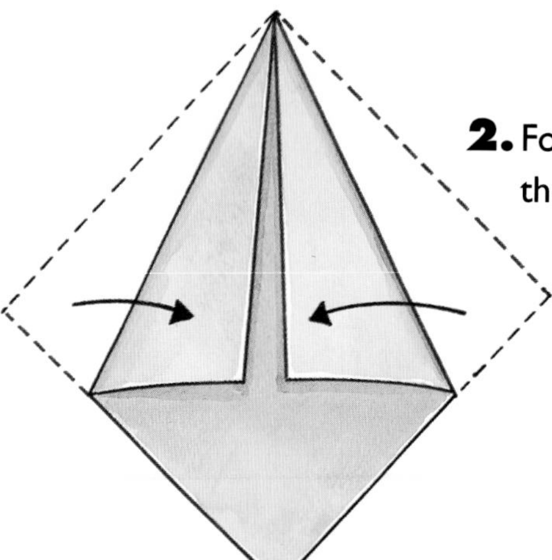

2. Fold the sides to the center.

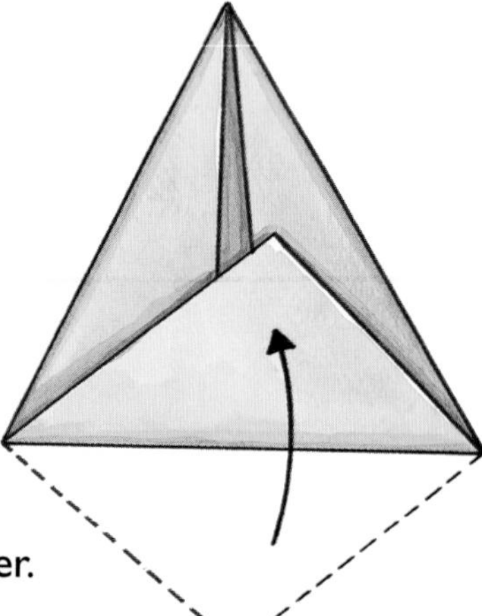

3. Fold the bottom up as shown. Now you have a triangle of paper.

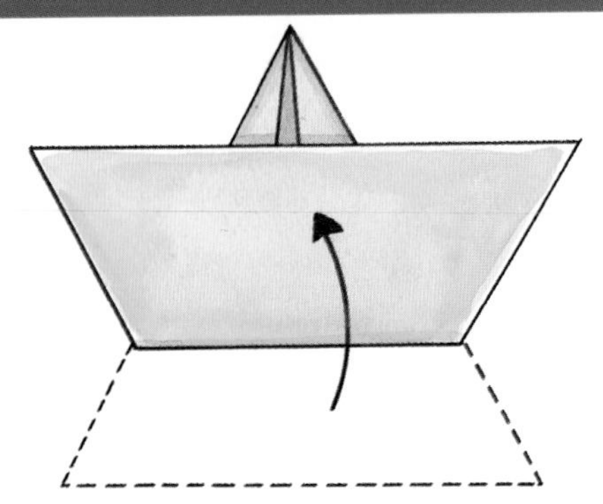

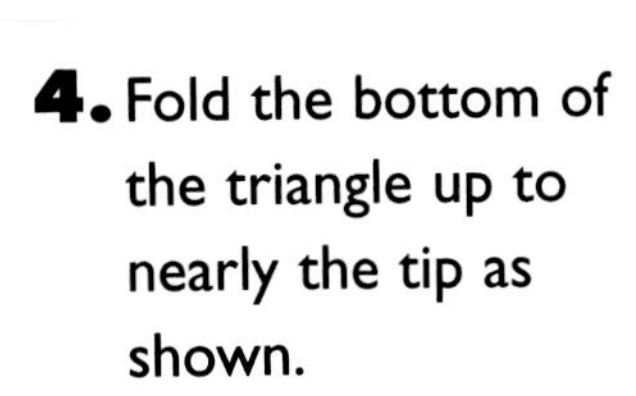

4. Fold the bottom of the triangle up to nearly the tip as shown.

5. Turn the paper over and fold the doll arms in toward the center as shown.

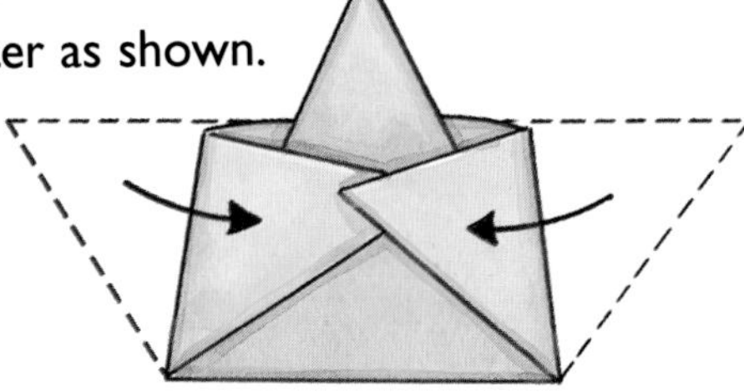

6. Fold the tip back. Then fold the base back to make the doll stand upright.

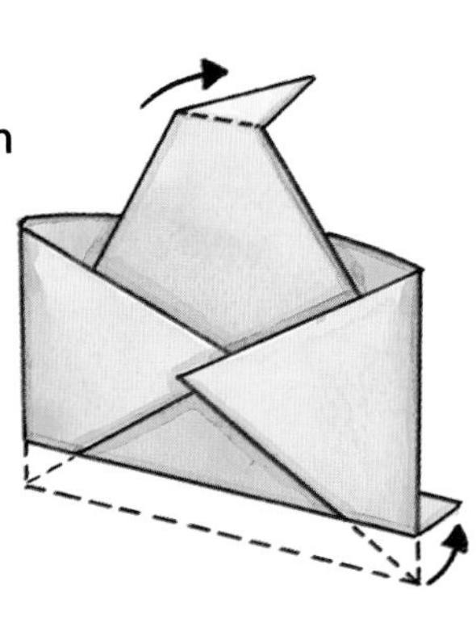

7. Draw a face on the doll and some designs on the body.

Carle's Collage Creatures

How can you spot Eric Carle's picture books? They have pictures made with colorful scraps of painted tissue papers, which he paints himself. The caterpillar in *The Very Hungry Caterpillar* is a **collage.**

To make the very hungry caterpillar, first Carle made a drawing of the caterpillar. He placed that drawing on top of a piece of red tissue paper and cut along the outline of the face. He put glue on the back of the tissue

The Very Hungry Caterpillar is a book of collage drawings.

face and stuck it to a white board. One by one, Carle cut out the other parts of the caterpillar and added them to the red face. Then he drew details, such as hairs, with crayon.

Eric Carle

In 1929, Eric Carle was born to German parents in Syracuse, New York. As a preschooler, Eric took many walks with his father. They often stopped to look under rocks and dead leaves. There they discovered tiny creatures, such as insects, spiders, and worms. Eric Carle's love of nature began with these walks.

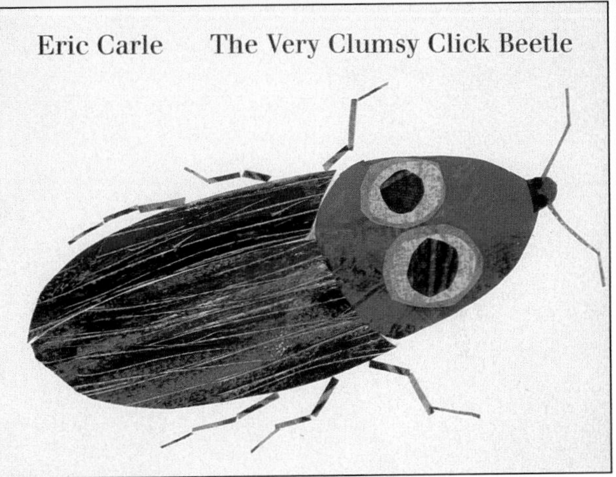

The Very Clumsy Click Beetle is another of Carle's books that combines his love of insects with collage.

Eric started school in Syracuse. He enjoyed experimenting with the fat brushes and bright paints in his art class. Eric's teacher saw that he had talent. She urged his mother to encourage his drawing. But he learned more about animals and art outside school than inside.

By first grade, Eric was living in Stuttgart, Germany. On summer visits to farms, Eric milked cows and watched bees. While in the city, he visited his Uncle August, a storyteller, who inspired the young Eric. Eric Carle went on to make up his own stories with the collage creatures that delight children and adults today.

Paper Cutting

**Cutting paper to make beautiful designs is a craft in many parts of the world. A kind of paper cutting called *papel picado* (puh PEHL pih KAH doh) is a popular craft in the Mexican state of Puebla. The markets there offer hundreds of scary and funny characters cut into paper banners. Mexicans hang papel picado banners on string to decorate their homes and shops. You, too, can cut paper and make a colorful decoration. Just follow these steps.

You Will Need:

- a light-colored pencil or crayon
- a sheet of heavy black paper
- scissors
- tissue paper in different colors
- glue or tape
- string

What To Do:

1. Draw a large fish or some other animal on the sheet of black paper.

2. Draw shapes on your animal. You need to make the shapes big enough to cut easily.

3. Cut out the animal and the inside shapes. To do this, you may fold the paper a little and make a small slit in the fold. Poke the blade of your scissors through the slit. Hold the scissors in one place and move the paper as you cut.

4. Cover the cutouts with different-colored tissue paper. Glue or tape the tissue in place.

5. Punch a hole in the top of your decoration and loop a string through the hole.

If you hang your paper cutout in front of a window, the light will shine through and brighten the room.

Make a Paper Lantern

You Will Need:

sheets of heavy paper in different colors
a pencil
a ruler
scissors
tape
tissue paper

A lantern is a case that covers a candle or light bulb. Usually it is made of glass or paper through which the light can shine. The Japanese use paper lanterns as colorful decorations. They even have a name for making lanterns—*kerigami* (KAIR uh GAH mee), the Japanese word for cutting paper. To make your own kerigami lanterns, follow these steps.

What To Do:

1. Fold one sheet of paper in half the long way. Draw a line the length of the paper about an inch from the edges away from the fold.

2. Cut slits about one-half inch (1 1/4 cm) apart up to this line. Unfold the slotted paper.

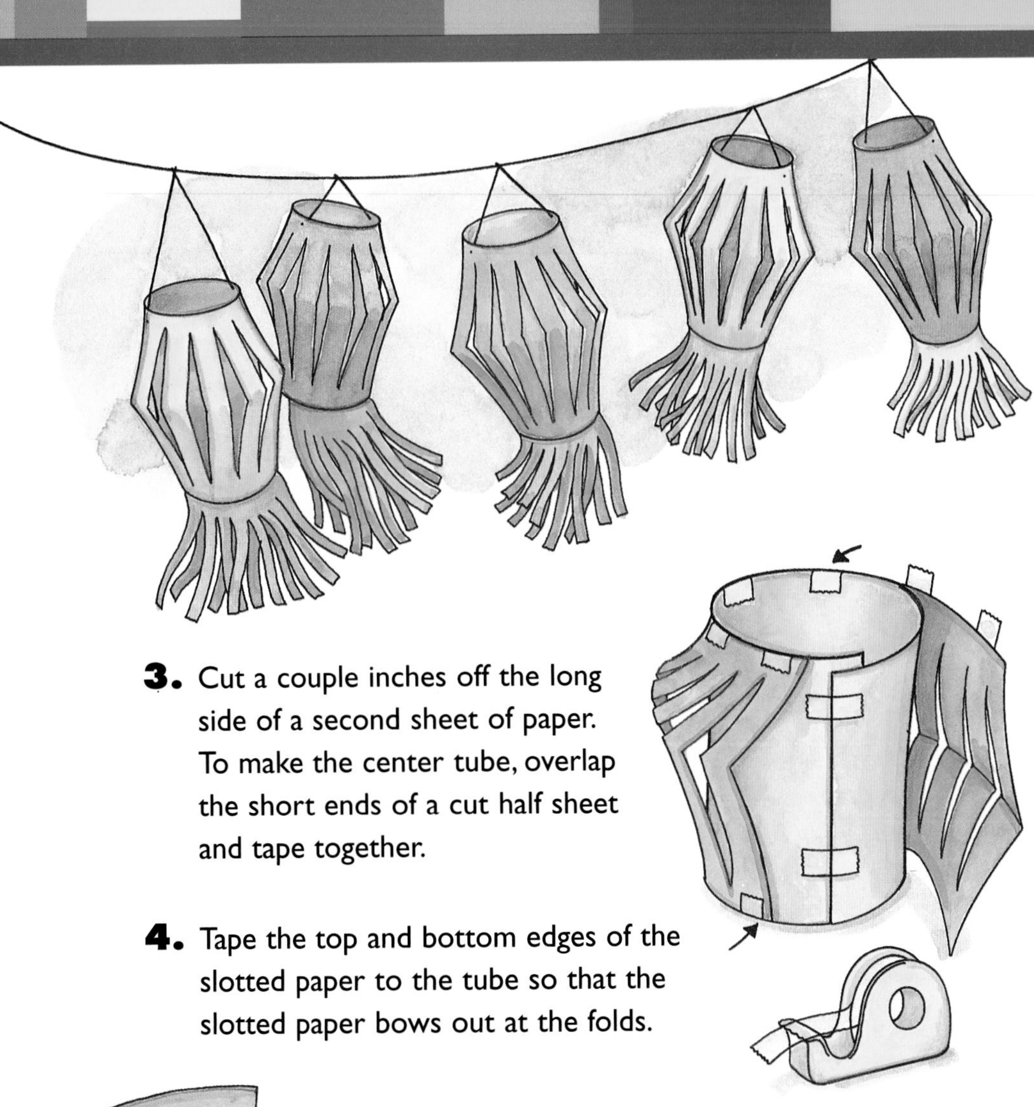

3. Cut a couple inches off the long side of a second sheet of paper. To make the center tube, overlap the short ends of a cut half sheet and tape together.

4. Tape the top and bottom edges of the slotted paper to the tube so that the slotted paper bows out at the folds.

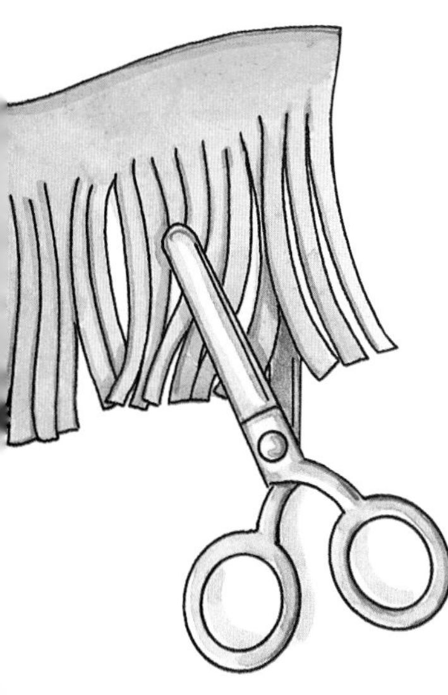

5. Fold a sheet of tissue paper with the short sides together. Cut the bottom edge with the fold to the left to make a fringe. Open the paper and tape it to the inside of the lantern as shown above.

Hang your lantern outdoors and watch the fringe wave in the breeze.

From Rags to Quilts

The first settlers in America had no factories or stores, and many communities had no craftworkers either. People had to build their own houses, grow their own food, and make their own clothing.

To make clothing, colonists had to do more than just cut out cloth and sew it together. First, they had to grow flax for linen and raise sheep for wool. Next, they had to spin the fibers into thread or yarn. Often they colored it in dyes made from boiled plants. Then they wove or knitted it into cloth.

When the colonists' handmade clothing became ragged, they didn't throw it away. They found other ways to use it. Some cloth was cut into patches and then pieced together to make blankets called patchwork **quilts** (kwihlts). The craft of quiltmaking is still popular today.

A quilt is a kind of fabric sandwich. The top and bottom layers are cloth. The filling is made of raw cotton or some other soft material.

Many craftworkers piece together patchwork quilts.

Today, quilters sew the layers together with tiny stitches. The top and bottom layers can be made out of many colored patches. Sometimes the stitches form designs like diamonds, leaves, or stars over the patches.

The Roots of Ringgold's Art

When you think of a painting, what do you see in your mind? A piece of canvas, painted and framed, hanging on a wall? That is probably what most people would think of. But artist Faith Ringgold makes paintings and other works of art by using materials in new ways.

Ringgold started experimenting with fabric in 1972, when she was teaching art at a college in New York City. At that time, Ringgold was insisting that museums show art by African American women. Much of this art was made of beads and fabric. Ringgold encouraged her students to use beads and fabric in their art. So why, asked a student, did Ringgold always use canvas and paint in her own work?

Faith Ringgold

The question made Ringgold wonder, too. After all, the women in her family had worked with fabric for almost 100 years. Her mother made a living by sewing and had taught Ringgold how to use a sewing machine.

But how could Ringgold mix fabric and painting? On a trip overseas, she discovered a way—*tankas* (TAHN kahs). These are cloth frames that Tibetans use on sacred paintings. Faith started framing her own paintings with tankas.

Next, Ringgold began making cloth sculptures. They looked like African masks. One such sculpture—*Mrs. Jones and Family*—shows Faith, her mother, Willi, her brother, Andrew, and her sister, Barbara, with their mouths wide open. The open mouths stand for the tradition of storytelling in Faith's family.

Ringgold worked quilting into her painting in 1986. She used an African design—squares of four triangles—to make a quilted border around her painting *Groovin' High*. She even quilted large squares onto the painted canvas.

Church Picnic by Faith Ringgold features a quilted border.

Use Batik to Color Cloth

People around the world have been dyeing cloth for thousands of years. In many places, special ways of dyeing developed. For example, in Indonesia the people use a method called ***batik*** (BUH teek).

You Will Need:

newspapers or cardboard
2 glass cake pans
food coloring (red and yellow)
hot water
white cotton cloth
tape
a white crayon

What To Do:

1. Cover your work area with newspaper. Mix a tablespoon of yellow food coloring and 1/2 cup (118 milliliters) of hot water in a cake pan. Soak the cloth in the pan. Remove the cloth and dry it.

2. Tape the dry cloth on the cardboard or newspaper. Then draw a design on the cloth with the white crayon.

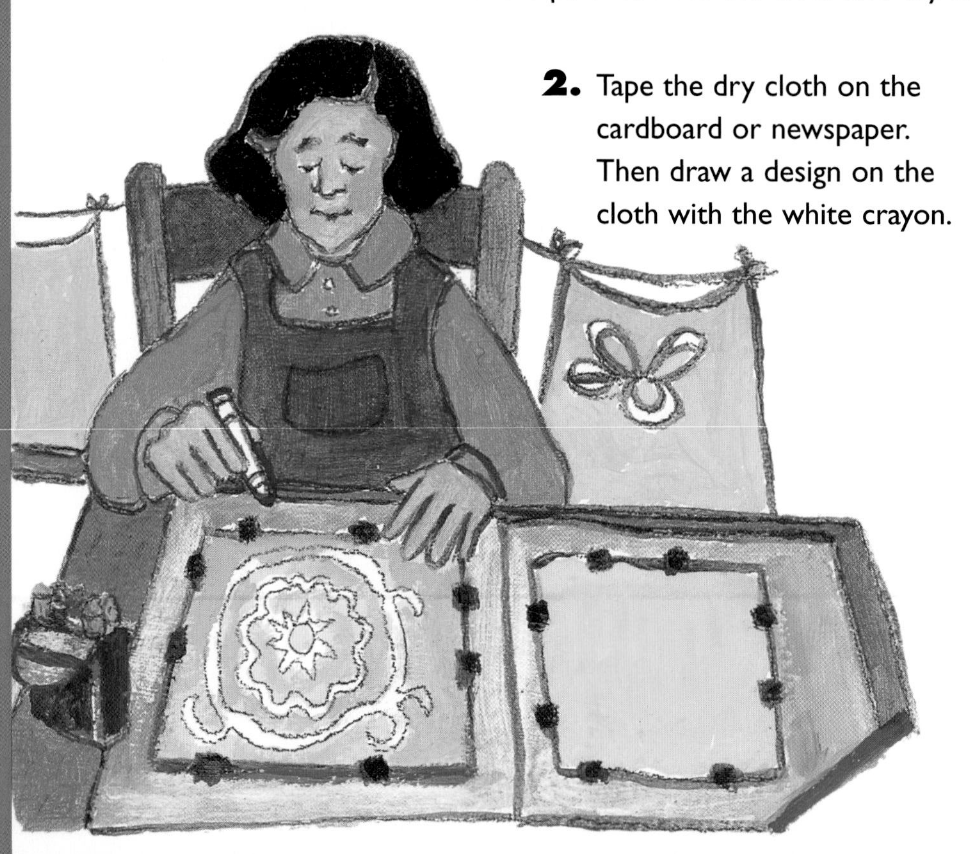

3. In the other cake pan, mix a tablespoon of red coloring with 1/2 cup (118 milliliters) of hot water. Soak the cloth in the red coloring. Then hang the fabric to dry.

You now have a batik design in yellow and orange. The wax of the crayon kept the red dye off the areas you drew on, so they stayed yellow. The red and yellow dye made orange on the other areas.

Weave a Paper Mat

The Samals are a group of people in the Philippines who weave beautiful mats. They use the leaves of the *pandanus* (pan DAY nuhs) plant, which grows all around them. You can weave a mat from materials around you, too. Try this mat made from magazine pages.

You Will Need:

8 colorful pages cut from large magazines
scissors
clear tape

What To Do:

1. Fold one double page lengthwise. Open it and cut it on the fold. Repeat this with the other pages to make 16 pieces.

2. Fold one piece in half lengthwise. Fold it in half lengthwise again. Press the paper firmly into a long flat strip. Fold and press the other pieces the same way.

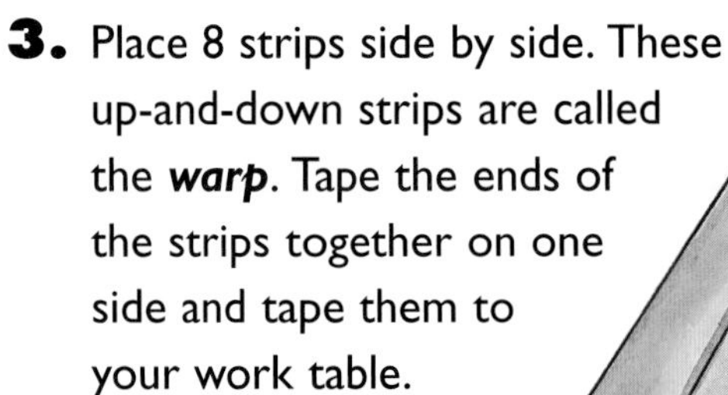

3. Place 8 strips side by side. These up-and-down strips are called the ***warp***. Tape the ends of the strips together on one side and tape them to your work table.

4. Weave the remaining strips over and under the taped ones. These strips that go across are called the ***weft***. The first, third, fifth, and seventh strips should go over and then under. The second, fourth, sixth, and eighth strips should go under and then over.

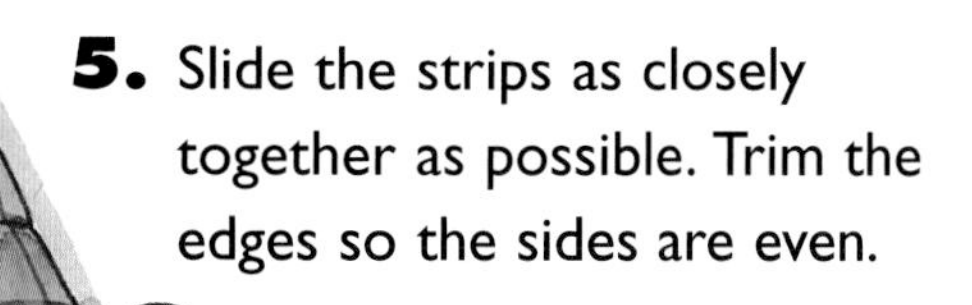

5. Slide the strips as closely together as possible. Trim the edges so the sides are even.

6. Finish your mat by taping the strips together on all four edges of your mat. Start with the side opposite the one that's taped to your work surface.

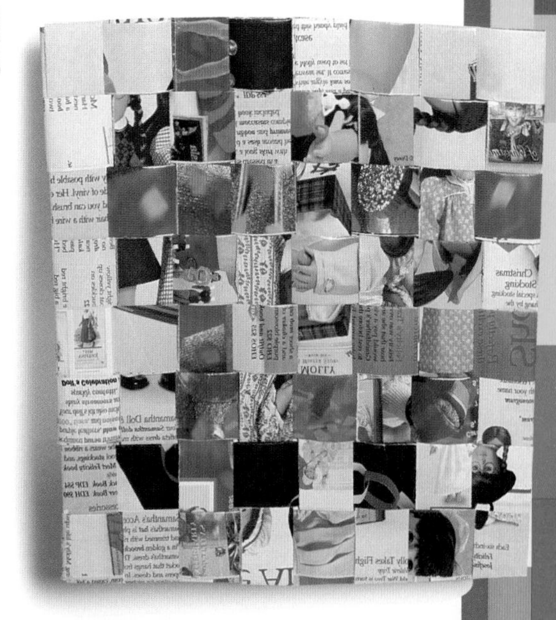

Use your artwork as a place mat at your next meal. Or display it where everyone can enjoy it.

Pressed Leaves and Flowers

Dried leaves and flowers can be used for all kinds of decorations. You can glue them onto stationery, put them in a pretty frame, or put them in homemade candles. Once you have a good collection, you can use it for craft projects all year around.

You Will Need:

leaves and flowers
newspaper
heavy books
wax paper
plain stationery and other paper
glue
iron

What To Do:

1. Place fresh leaves and flowers between sheets of newspaper.

2. Press the leaves and flowers by placing some heavy books on top of the newspaper. Wait at least one week for the plants to dry. If you write the date on the newspaper, you will know when the plants should be ready.

3. Place each plant between two sheets of waxed paper. Ask an adult to iron the leaves and flowers on both sides. The wax will help the pressed leaves and flowers keep their shape.

4. You are now ready to use your pressed plants on all sorts of things. Have fun!

Glue your dried flowers to decorate place mats, stationery, and notecards.

In Stitches

There are huge machines in factories that sew most of our clothes and other items. But many people still enjoy sewing by hand or with their own sewing machines. One reason people like to sew their own clothes is because, that way, they can choose exactly what size, color, and material they want. Some people like to sew special things for their homes, such as curtains or pillows. People also sew gifts for their friends or families.

Embroidery is a kind of sewing craft that uses stitches to make pictures or designs.

Embroidery (ihm BROY duh ree) is a craft that is related to sewing. It is used mainly for decoration. A person who embroiders uses a special needle and colored thread called embroidery floss to make different kinds of stitches on cloth. The stitches can form pictures or designs.

You may have a shirt or sweater with words or pictures on it that have been embroidered by a machine. But many craftworkers enjoy embroidering by hand because it is creative and it relaxes them.

Embroidery basics

Before you embroider, practice basic stitching.

You Will Need:

- a loosely woven cloth
- embroidery floss (from a fabric or arts and crafts store)
- scissors
- an embroidery needle
- an embroidery hoop
- a pencil

What To Do:

1. Cut a piece of floss as long as your arm from fingertips to elbow. Moisten one end and push it through the eye of the needle. Tie a knot as shown below in the other end of the floss.

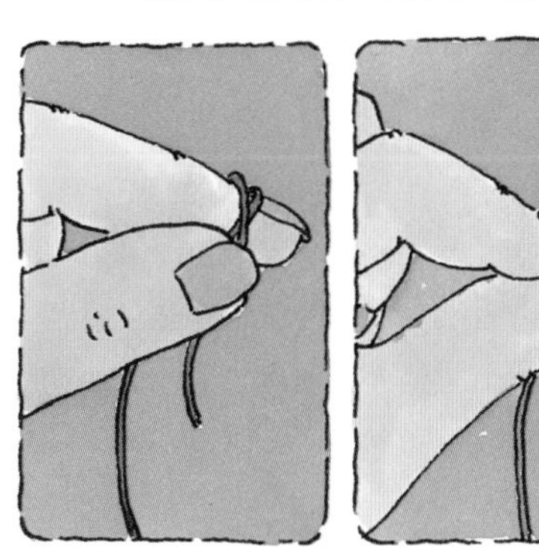

2. Push the needle up through the cloth that you've put between the two parts of the embroidery hoop. Pull the needle out on the other side until all the floss but the knot comes through. Then push the needle back down and pull the floss through. That is one stitch. Make a row of stitches all the same length.

3. When you are almost at the end of your floss, push the needle through to the back of the cloth. Make two small stitches, one on top of the other. Slide the needle under the stitches and pull the floss through. Cut the floss.

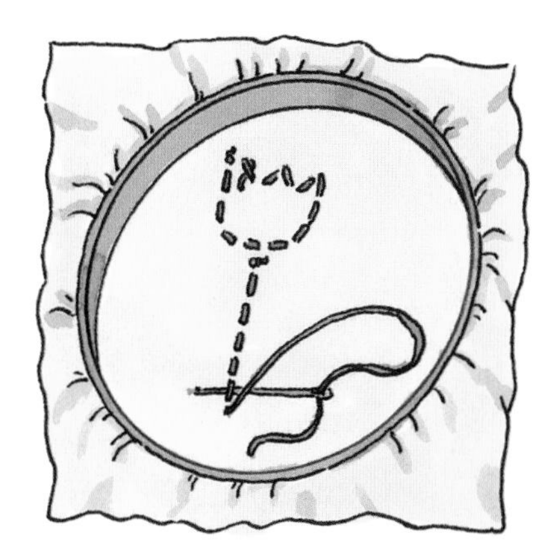

Learn to Embroider

You Will Need:

a loosely woven cloth
embroidery floss
scissors
an embroidery needle
an embroidery hoop
a pencil

Why did colonial women do so much embroidery or make so many decorations with needlework? They used it to cover holes and rips in old clothing and linens while decorating the cloth at the same time. You, too, can do embroidery to make cloth as pretty as a picture.

What To Do:

1. Place your cloth in an embroidery hoop.

2. On the cloth, draw a design with large and small flowers. Then embroider the design with the following stitches.

3. Use the satin stitch for filling in large petals and leaves.

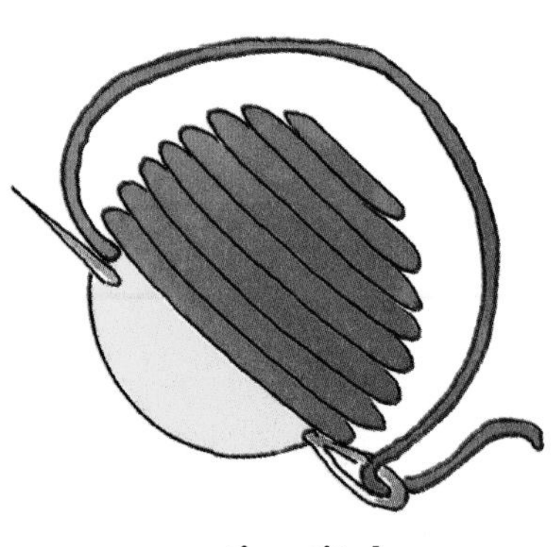

satin stitch

4. Use the chain stitch to make stems.

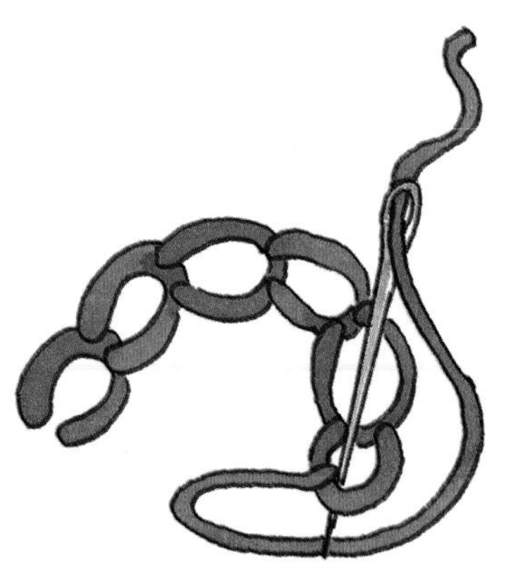

chain stitch

5. Use the lazy-daisy stitch to outline tiny petals and leaves.

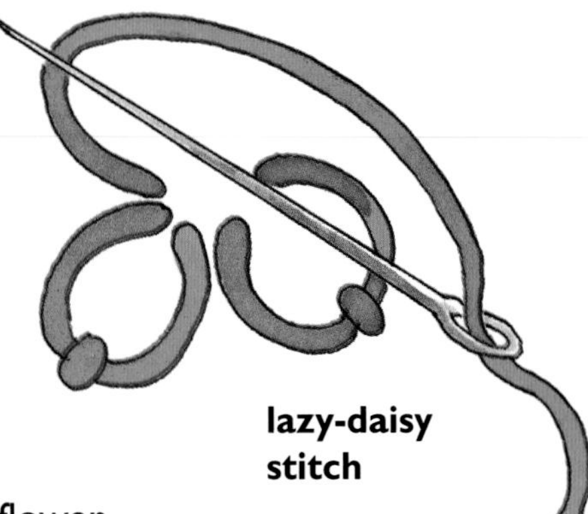

6. Knotted stitches, like these in the flower centers below, are easy to make. Wrap the floss around the point of the needle three times. Push the needle with the loops back in next to the hole.

Let's Paint

What feelings can you show in a painting? In a painting of a stormy sea, you can show the power of nature. In a quiet forest scene, you can express peace. A picture of food can send a message of plenty. Or a painting of empty bowls may say "hunger."

What can you express in a painting that doesn't show anything real, like people or objects? You can use colors and designs to show feelings. You can express your own feelings this way.

Prehistoric Paintings

Imagine living more than 30,000 years ago. Writing has not been invented yet. But you want to keep track of the exciting things that happen to you. How do you do it?

Very early people used pictures to record their adventures. In 1956, Frenchman Henri Lhote discovered hundreds of paintings on cave walls in Algeria. Many of them show different kinds of animals. They also show people doing everyday things, such as hunting and herding animals.

Thousands of years ago, the native people of Australia painted pictures on bark. Their relatives who live in Australia today, the Aborigines, still paint bark pictures. Most of these pictures tell stories that were passed down from parents to children for hundreds of years.

To make a bark picture, Aborigines cut bark from a eucalyptus (YOOK kuh lihp tuhs) tree. Next, they flatten

Prehistoric people made cave paintings about 30,000 years ago. Cave paintings were one of the earliest forms of art.

These animal paintings were found in a cave in 1940 by some boys near their home in Lascaux, France. They were painted by people who lived thousands of years ago.

and dry the bark. Then they scratch a design into the bark and paint the design. They make their paint from crushed plants mixed with charcoal.

Jars, Tubes, and Powders

Paints come in a rainbow of colors. Some paints are runny and come in jars. Other paints are oozy and come in tubes. Still other paints come in solids or powders. You have to add water before you can use them.

The kinds of paints you probably use most are water colors, temperas (TEHM puhr uhz), and powder paints. All these paints are made of pigments and binders. A pigment is a powder that gives the paint its color. A binder makes the pigments stick together.

Water colors are probably the easiest paints to use. They come in tubes or solid tablets. You add a little water if you want the paint's color to be strong, and more water if you want a thin paint with a delicate color.

Tempera paints are also easy to use. They are thicker than water colors.

Temperas are ready to use and clean up fast with soap and water. But they cost more than other paints.

Powder paints may be thick or thin, depending on how much water you add. For a thick paint with a shiny finish, mix the powder with white glue. This shiny paint works great for finger painting.

Making Potstone Paint

If you want to paint a picture, you do not need to buy paint. You and an adult can make some at home.

You Will Need:

plain talcum powder
liquid soap
liquid starch
corn syrup
3 plastic cups
one or more paintbrushes
several sheets of plain paper
food coloring

What To Do:

1. Put liquid soap in a plastic cup. Put liquid starch in another plastic cup. Put corn syrup in a third plastic cup.

2. Mix enough talcum powder into each liquid to make it thick and light colored.

3. Make different colors. Add a few drops of food coloring to the first cup and then stir. Add a few drops of a different color to the next cup. Add drops of another color to the third cup.

paint formulas

Now you are ready to paint! Paint a simple design or picture with each kind of paint. See how long the paint takes to dry. Notice how it looks when dry. Is it thick or thin, smooth or rough, dull or shiny?

Make Your Own Palette

You Will Need:

- an old shirt
- a sponge
- newspaper
- an aluminum pie tin
- red, yellow, and blue paint
- 3 spoons
- cotton swabs
- plain paper

Artists often arrange their colors on a board called a palette. They always put each color in the same spot, so they know exactly where to find it. You can make your own palette with just three colors—red, blue, and yellow! These are called **primary colors**. All other colors can be made from the three primary colors. Try this yourself.

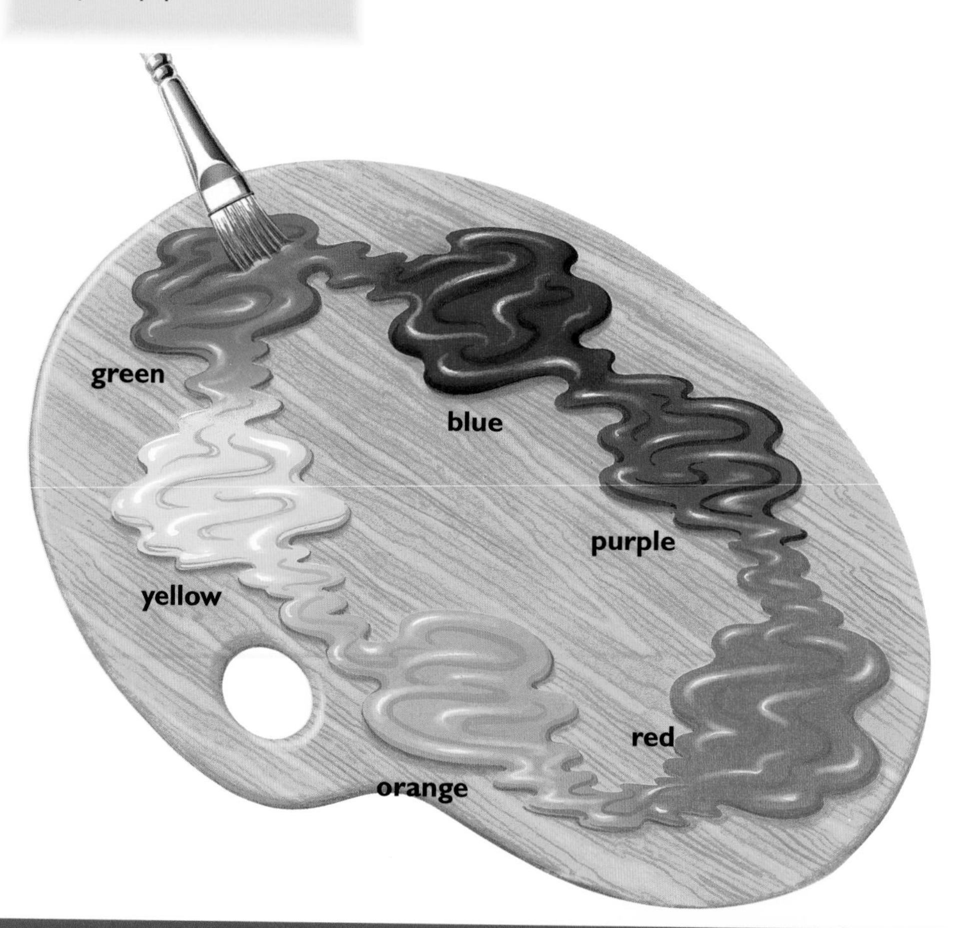

What To Do:

1. First, get ready to paint. Wear an old shirt to protect your clothing. Keep a sponge handy in case of spills. Cover your entire work area with newspaper.

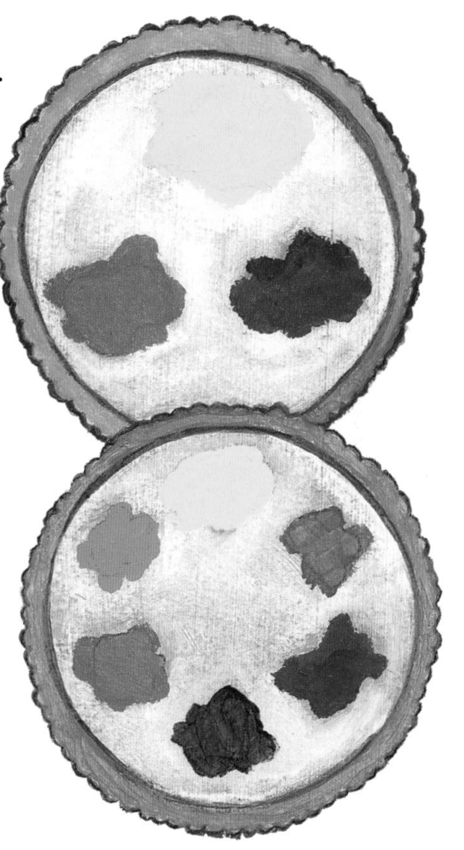

2. Put a spoon in each of the three colors of paint. Spoon some of each color onto the pie tin. This is your basic palette.

3. With a cotton swab, blend a small amount of red and yellow. Then with a clean swab, blend yellow and blue. Then mix blue and red with another swab. What colors do you get? Orange, green, and purple are called **secondary colors.**

4. Experiment with your palette of colors. Try mixing a little more red or a little more yellow with orange. What happens? What happens when you add more blue or more yellow to green? What happens when you add more blue or red to purple?

   Pick your favorite colors from your palette and paint a picture on the paper.

The Color of Shadows

In the 1870's in France, a group of painters called impressionists (ihm PREHSH uhn ihsts) invented a new style of painting. New kinds of packaging helped make this new style of painting possible. Lead tubes kept paint from drying out. Now painters could work outside their studios. They took their easels, canvases, and brushes, and painted outdoors.

Outdoors, in natural light, impressionists noticed that objects cast colored shadows. So they painted orange haystacks with blue shadows, red dresses with green shadows, and yellow pots with purple shadows.

The colors they were seeing in shadows are called complementary colors. They are like color opposites. To help identify colors in light and shadow, many artists use color charts. You can make your own chart of primary, secondary, and complementary colors.

Complementary colors are used in this painting called *Hoarfrost* by Camille Pissaro. Which do you see?

Here's a picture of a color palette. To find complementary colors, look for colors that are opposite each other on the palette. For example, yellow is the complementary color for purple. What is the complementary color for orange?

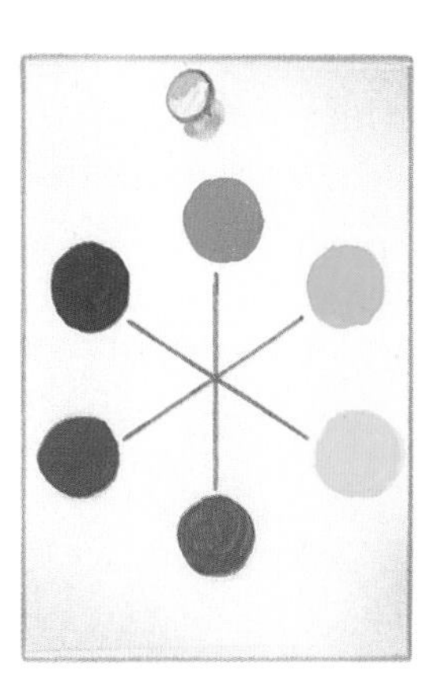

Tints and Shades

How would you describe the color of the sky on a clear day? Most people would say it is blue. But perhaps the sky is not as blue as it was yesterday. Or maybe it is bluer than the sea or a river. There are so many kinds of blue! What makes one blue different from another?

If you have paints, try adding white to some colors. You'll find that red turns pink, purple turns lavender, and dark blue turns light blue. Colors with white added are called tints.

Now try mixing your colors with a little black to see how they change. Black makes colors darker. These darker colors are called shades.

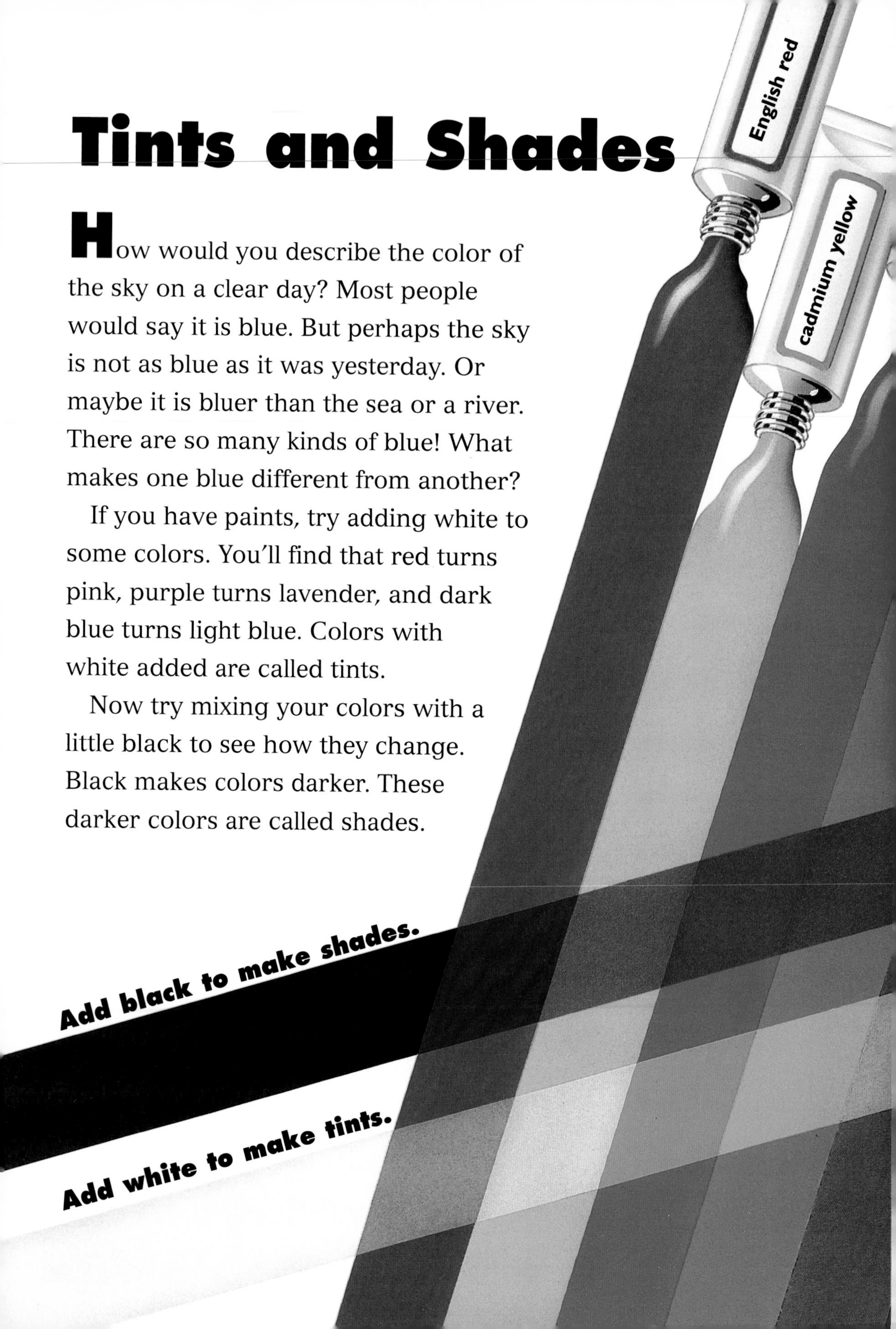

All colors—
red, yellow, blue,
orange, green,
purple, and the
colors in between—
have many tints and
shades. Blacks and
whites even come in
different tints and shades,
with interesting names like
Mars black or zinc white.

Out of the Blue

At first glance, this picture might look like streaks of color splashed over the page. But the painter, Nazli Madkour, wanted to create more than a pretty pattern. She wanted to tell you about something that she saw. Let's think about what it could be.

Nazli Madkour

Look at the pale, cool colors. Maybe the colors are telling you about a special place. Could it be somewhere cool?

The colors seem to rush here and there across one another. Could the picture show something that is moving fast?

See the splash of blue in the lower-right corner? Blue has a calming effect. Does the blue in this painting make you feel calm?

Now look at the dark lines and shapes. Do you see things in motion? Can you see a bird flying?

A painting should set you wondering and guessing. Maybe the artist painted the wind the way she did to make you think. She wanted you to see calm in the midst of motion. Perhaps she thought you would imagine how it would feel to be a bird in flight.

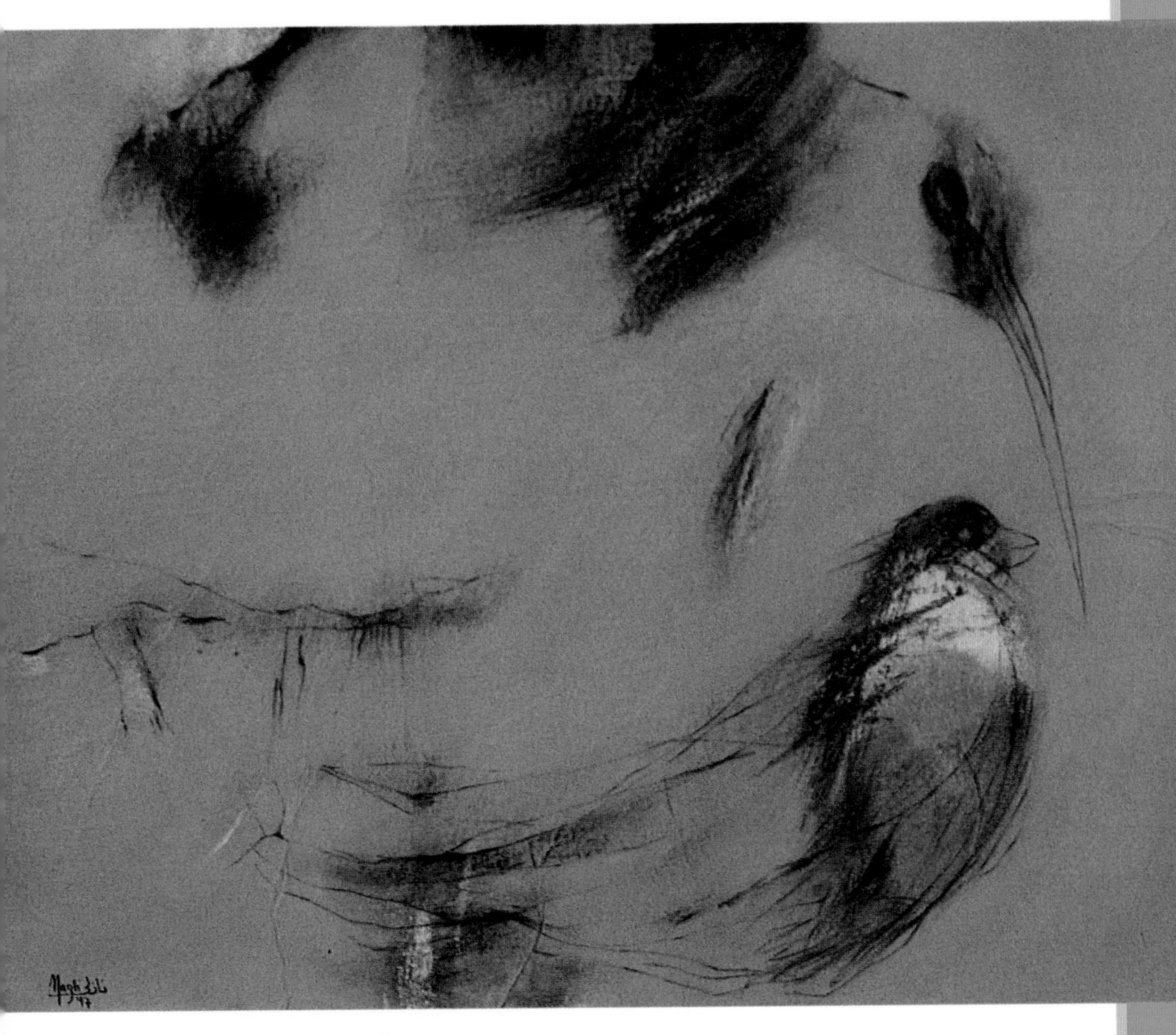

Nazli Madkour, from Egypt, painted this picture titled *Caring*.

A Lasting Impression

Sometimes artists leave out the details in a painting to create a feeling. Half-close your eyes and look at this painting. You can almost feel the sunshine poking through the treetops and warming the forest floor.

Impressionist Berthe Morisot painted this scene of a forest, called *Foret de Compiegne*.

This is a photo of a forest. How does the impressionist painting make you feel compared to the photo? Does it give you the "feeling" of a forest the way a photo does?

Now look at the picture closely. It does not show much detail. You cannot see the bark on the trees or even the kinds of trees in the forest. The artist has painted only an impression of the scene.

In the close-up photo above, you can see all the details of a forest. It looks as if the camera captured every pine needle! But when you see a forest in one quick look, you do not see all the detail. You see it like the painter did—a blurry impression of color, light, and shade.

A painting does not always need lots of detail. The colors can make an impression of a scene without all the details that show up in a photo.

Light and Dark

Artists perform a kind of magic using light and dark. They use them to grab your attention.

Suppose an artist wants you to notice a certain part of a painting. A good way to do this is to make that part a light color and surround it with a dark color. The result is called **contrast**.

Marc Chagall used a lot of contrast to paint *The Praying Jew.*

In this picture, the painter used contrast to draw your eyes to the center. He painted a white shawl on a man dressed mostly in black. Since white reflects a lot of light, the white shawl stands out well.

Suppose an artist wants you to notice a subject's shape instead of his or her face and clothing. The artist might paint the person in front of a light. The result would be a dark shape against a light background. This kind of picture is called a **silhouette** (SIHL oo eht).

In the picture below, the painter placed the girl in front of the light. Her silhouette stands out against the sky. The artist used light and dark to give you a surprising view of an ordinary scene.

TRY THIS! 1

Look at the pictures and posters at home and school. What catches your eye? Do the artists play tricks with dark and light?

***Morning Light* by Caspar David Friedrich**

Putting it in Perspective

How do artists do it? They paint their pictures on flat surfaces, but we seem to see deep into the pictures. Why? Because the artists use **perspective** (puhr SPEHK tihv).

In real life, street lights down the road look like they are smaller than nearby street lights. Artists try to get this effect in their painting with perspective. This means they paint some things small and short to show that they are supposed to be far away.

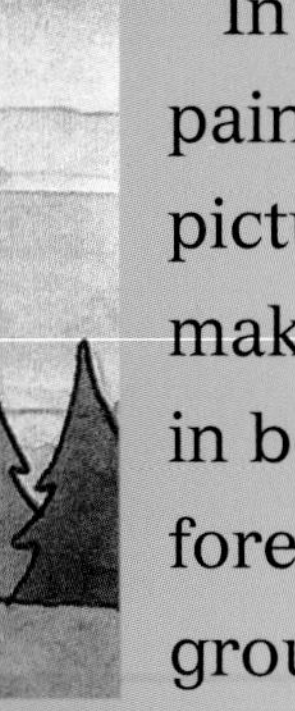

Compare the larger tree in the foreground of this picture to the smaller ones in the back. This gives the painting depth.

In the same picture, the artist paints everything at the front of the picture larger. These larger things make up the foreground. Everything in between the background and the foreground makes up the middle ground. Having a foreground, a middle ground, and a background gives a painting depth, or perspective.

Artists use even more tricks to give their paintings depth. Sometimes they paint the background pale and misty.

In his painting *Paris-Auteuil,* Maurice Utrillo shows perspective by making the buildings in the background smaller. He also makes the street narrower.

This makes the background look far away. Other times, they draw the straight lines in a street or road so they meet in the background. This makes the road seem to disappear in the distance just as a real road appears to do.

Straight lines in this picture meet in the background. This gives a feeling of distance.

Mary Cassatt's Impressions of Women

Why don't we see more paintings from long ago done by women? Before the middle 1800's, art schools did not accept women students. One of the first women to go to art school was the American painter Mary Cassatt.

When Mary was 16, in 1861, she entered the Pennsylvania Academy of Fine Arts in Philadelphia. Many considered the academy daringly modern because it admitted women. But Mary thought its classes were boring, even though she studied there for four years.

Mary Cassatt painted this picture of herself around 1880.

In the mid-1800's, most Americans considered art unimportant. Cassatt wanted people to take her paintings seriously. So in 1866, she moved to Paris.

Cassatt's first paintings showed people in dark colors. Then she saw the work of Edgar Degas, an impressionist. Degas's pictures were a turning point in her life as an artist.

Cassatt started painting with light, bright colors. She used dabs of paint to create the "impression" of a scene rather than an exact copy. Like the other impressionists, she showed only what the eye saw at a glance and how light changed the color.

The people in Cassatt's new paintings looked natural. Her most popular works show mothers and children. Other paintings picture women at peaceful activities like sewing and reading.

By the time Mary Cassatt died in 1926, Americans admired her paintings as much as Europeans did. Within two years after her death, Americans put on four exhibits, or showings, of her work. The largest exhibit was in Philadelphia, where Cassatt first studied art.

Mary Cassatt often painted natural scenes of women involved in peaceful activities, as in *The Boating Party.*

Stringing Along

Brushes and paints are not the only tools painters use. They also make imaginative use of things that seem very ordinary. Try your hand at using string to make extraordinary designs.

You Will Need:

3 spoons
tempera paint in 3 colors
3 small containers (Ask an adult for ones that are okay to put paint in.)
scissors
a ball of string
2 large sheets of newsprint or package wrapping
an old shirt
newspaper

What To Do:

1. Put on the old shirt to protect your clothes. Cover your workspace with newspaper. Spoon one color of paint into each container.

2. Cut three pieces of string, each about half as long as your arm.

3. Hold a piece of string by one end and dip the other end into one of the paints. Make certain the string is covered with paint. Dip a piece of string in each container.

4. Pull a string out of the paint. Hold the string by one end and drop the rest of it onto a sheet of paper. Lift the string and drop it on another part of the paper. The paint-covered string will make wiggly designs.

5. Do the same with all the different-colored strings.

6. Now fold another sheet of paper in half with a painted string inside. While gently pressing the folded paper with one hand, slowly pull the string out with the other. Open the paper.

See the original designs you can make without even looking!

Breath and Finger Painting

What painting tools does everybody have and yet they cannot be bought? Breath and fingers. Follow these steps to paint with your breath.

You Will Need:

sheets of white paper
newspaper
3 spoons
finger paint in 3 colors (See the recipes for potstone paint on page 44.)
drinking straws
an old shirt

To Paint With Your Breath:

1. Put on the old shirt to protect your clothes. Cover your work space with newspaper. Lay a spoonful of paint on a sheet of the white paper.

2. Place one end of the straw near the paint. Blow gently through the other end to spread out the paint.

Give a straw to a friend and "blow" a picture together.

3. Put the other colors on the paper, and blow them around, too. Use a clean spoon for each color.

4. When you finish your picture, put the paper on newspaper to dry.

To Paint With Your Fingers:

1. Put on an old shirt to protect your clothing. Spread out the newspaper and put the white sheet of paper on top.

2. Spoon some paint onto the white paper.

3. Use your hands to spread the paint over the paper. Make patterns using your fingertips and fingernails. Let the painting dry.

Display your paintings with pride. After all, you put a lot of yourself into them!

Pictures Good Enough to Eat

The French artist Nicolas Poussin thought that in a painting, details were more important than color. So did many other artists of the 1600's. Poussin also believed that painting should show only serious subjects. So Poussin based many of his pictures on legends and the Bible. The painting, *Holy Family on the Steps,* shows the family with a basket of apples. In the 1600's, a basket of apples was a symbol for life. The apples may also make us think of

***Holy Family on the Steps,* by a follower of Poussin**

This detail of the painting shows a basket of apples. What do the apples mean to you?

Curtain, Carafe and Plate of Fruit, **by Paul Cézanne**

the Bible story of Eve tempting Adam with an apple in the garden of Eden.

In 1877, the French artist Paul Cézanne painted the plate of apples shown on this page. Unlike Poussin's work, Cézanne's work was not popular during his lifetime. He learned art from the impressionists, but he used perspective in his paintings in a way that the impressionists never did. His style inspired modern artists, including Pablo Picasso of Spain.

Compare the paintings. If Poussin's apples are "serious," how would you describe Cézanne's apples? Which apples look more real? Which apples seem to say, "Have a bite"?

You're the Artist

Look closely at the painting on this page. You see dots instead of brushstrokes. The French painter Georges Seurat used dots to make this painting, *The Bathers at Asnières*. See how the dog's shadow on the grass is a mixture of black and green dots? Notice how the dots of blue and brown combine to make sunlight on the water. Can you find other parts in this portion of the painting where different-colored dots suggest sun and shade?

You Will Need:

- a coloring book
- tracing paper
- brushes
- water colors

You can make pictures with dots, too. Try it. Just use Seurat's style of painting on a picture of your own.

What To Do:

1. Pick a favorite picture from the coloring book. Place the tracing paper over the picture.

2. "Trace" the picture by painting a dot about every 1/2 inch (1.3 centimeters) along the outline. Then fill the spaces with dots.

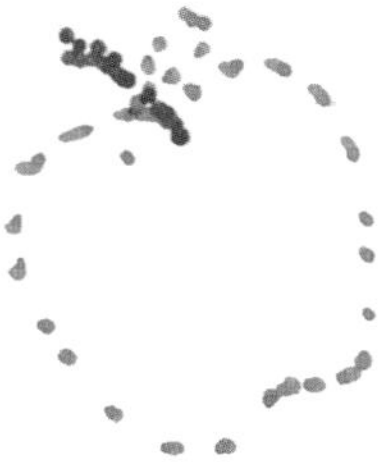

3. Try placing the dots far apart. Then try placing them close together. Use yellow dots or white spaces with colored dots to show light. Use black and colored dots to show shade. Try shadows in complementary colors, too.

The Tale of Beatrix Potter

Beatrix Potter spent most of her childhood in a tall, stone house in London. In the late 1800's, young women called governesses taught girls from rich families at home. So Beatrix did not go to school and meet other children her age.

Beatrix Potter

The Potters' servants were Beatrix's friends. Her nurse told her fairy tales, and her governess taught her about flowers and plants. Cox, the butler, brought her animals that she kept in her third-floor schoolroom.

Two of Beatrix's dearest pets were mice that Cox caught in the Potters' kitchen. Beatrix named them Hunca Munca and Appley Dappley. She also kept a rabbit named Benjamin Bunny and fed him off a china plate. Her most unusual pet was probably Tiggy, a hedgehog, who drank milk from a teacup.

Beatrix Potter liked to draw sketches of her pet animals, including Benjamin Bunny.

Beatrix loved to watch her animals. She drew stacks of sketches showing Hunca Munca, Tiggy, and Benjamin Bunny in their favorite poses. For each drawing, Beatrix made up a story. She shared her stories with her governess after each day's lessons.

Beatrix's favorite season was summer, when the Potters visited the Scottish countryside. There Beatrix admired fields full of plants and animals. She drew the many wildflowers and animals that she saw and painted her drawings with water colors.

fur, I think he would be
more comfortable if he had

a little coat which would take
off. I shall send this to
Wandsworth, I daresay it will be sent
on to Ipswich, if you have not
come home. I remain
yours affectionately
Beatrix Potter
The little foal belongs to my uncle, it is so
tame.

Beatrix Potter wrote letters to her governess's children with stories and drawings of Peter Rabbit.

When Beatrix grew up, she remained good friends with her last governess. Beatrix visited her and wrote letters to her governess's children. One of the earliest letters was actually a story about a rabbit called Peter. It included drawings of the rabbit and his three sisters.

A publishing house offered to print the story as a book if Beatrix would color the pictures. So she brightened the drawings with delicate water colors. *The Tale of Peter Rabbit* became a huge success. In time, children all around the world were enjoying stories and water colors of Peter, Hunca Munca, Jemima Puddle-Duck, and a host of other animals that flowed from Beatrix Potter's brush.

Peter Rabbit is one of Beatrix Potter's beloved water color animals.

Working with Water Colors

Beatrix Potter drew just enough detail to give her drawings shape and texture, as in her water color of a cat sleeping in a garden, *below*. Then she used just the right tints, or colors, to bring them alive. How well can you blend lines and color? Find out. Paint a water color backdrop for a story about field mice. Try to create several tints from each color by changing the amount of water on your brush.

You Will Need:

- a pencil
- paintbrushes
- water colors
- water
- sheets of white drawing paper

What To Do:

1. Use a pencil to sketch a picture of a sky over a farm field. Show a sunrise, a sunset, a storm, or any other kind of outdoor scene you can imagine.

2. Add just a little water to paints to make deep colors. Add more water to create pale tints. Apply each color with a clean brush.

3. Use your brush to soften the lines between blocks of color on your drawing. Make each color seem to fade into the next.

4. Allow the paint to dry.

Display your finished water color for everyone to admire.

Make Your Own Animal Art

Here's how to create your own exotic animals, display animal art on the wall, and make a folding aquarium. Make animals like the ones shown here or create your own.

You Will Need:

powder or tempera paints
paintbrushes
2 small Styrofoam cups
3 large Styrofoam cups
cardboard
string
a hole puncher
glue
scissors

Fix Yourself a "Tweet":

1. Glue the two small cups together to make the bird's head. When the glue dries, paint eyes on the top cup and a beak on the bottom cup.

2. Glue the two large cups together to make the body. When the glue is dry, paint the feathers and wings with short brushstrokes.

3. Cut off the bottom of the third large cup. Glue the bottom of the body to use as a stand for the bird. When the glue is dry, paint bird feet on the stand.

Hang with the Animals:

1. Cut a large oval or triangle out of cardboard.

2. Punch holes on the right and left sides of the shape. Connect the holes with a string.

3. Paint the face of a tiger, fox, or some other animal on the cardboard.

4. Hang the picture from its string on the wall.

Get in the Swim:

1. Paint a scene from the ocean bottom on a large piece of cardboard. You can paint real sea creatures or create your own.

2. Fold the cardboard in thirds so it will stand up like a folding screen.

To create a wildlife park in your room, display your fantasy creatures.

Statues and Sculptures

What is sculpture? Sculpture is art you can walk around and view from many sides. People have been making sculptures for thousands of years.

Long ago, sculptors carved many figures from stone, bone, and wood. They modeled others in metal and clay. Sculptors today still work with these materials. But they may also use wax, paper, fabric, string, or plastic. Any material you can think of has probably been used for sculpture.

China's Terra-Cotta Army

China's first emperor lies in a tomb outside the city of Xian in eastern China. The emperor is not alone. Buried nearby are thousands of **terra-cotta** (TEHR uh KAHT uh) soldiers and their horses. They were created more than 2,200 years ago.

Terra cotta is clay that has been fired, or hardened, in an oven called a kiln. Large solid pieces of terra cotta would shrink and crack. So figures like the bodies of the Chinese soldiers are usually hollow.

The figures represent all branches of the early Chinese army—archers, cavalry, charioteers, and foot soldiers. And, out of 7,000 statues, no two faces look the same. Each is a life-sized portrait of a real person. The heads must have been sculpted one by one.

Thousands of terra-cotta soldiers stand guard at the tomb of China's first emperor.

Terra-Cotta Statues

Today, the emperor's terra-cotta army is kept in a large museum. Museum artists have a workshop where they make copies of the soldiers. As much as possible, these artists follow the steps the emperor's sculptors used more than 2,200 years ago.

First, an artist forms long ropes from clay. To build a soldier's body, the artist coils these ropes around and around. Next, the artist places one hand inside the body to steady it. With the other hand, he or she beats the coils together with a paddle.

The artists make the hands, ears, and basic head shapes in molds. They cover each molded head with a layer of clay. In this clay, they model the features of each soldier by hand. They use clay modeling tools to add details on the armor.

Workers then put the body parts in a kiln with a low fire. When the parts dry, the kiln's temperature rises to 1800 °F (1000 °C). The statues are baked until they glow red.

An artist works on a replica of a terra-cotta warrior in a workshop in Xian, China.

Making Play Clay

One of the most fun-to-use craft materials is clay. To make your own claylike dough, follow this recipe.

You Will Need:

- a saucepan
- 1 cup flour
- 1/2 cup salt
- 1 cup water
- 1 tablespoon oil
- 1 teaspoon cream of tartar
- food coloring
- a pastry board
- plastic bag that seals closed

What To Do:

1. Mix the flour, salt, water, oil, and cream of tartar in the saucepan.

2. Ask an adult to cook the mixture over low heat until thick. Then add food coloring until the dough is the color you want.

3. Let the dough cool. Then, place it on a board. Work it back and forth with your knuckles and palms.

4. Store the dough in a closed plastic bag at room temperature.

When you are ready to sculpt, your "clay" will be ready, too.

Playing with Clay

Clay
is a clown
with no bones.

No roll,
stretch,
split—
no feat of change
is too great
for it.

Pinch
a thin nose,
a chin.

Gouge
two eyeholes.
Chisel
a grin.

Would you then
pummel him flat,
thumb him again?

No!
He's become
someone.

Let's Play with Clay

Playing with clay is fun! Clay feels good. You feel good, too, as you push and squeeze the clay into shapes.

You Will Need:

clay
a baking sheet
a rolling pin
toothpick
an old hair comb
a pen
pencil
cookie cutters

What To Do:

1. Work your clay on a baking sheet. This way, you can easily move your finished model somewhere to dry.

2. Flatten the clay with the palm of your hand or with a rolling pin.

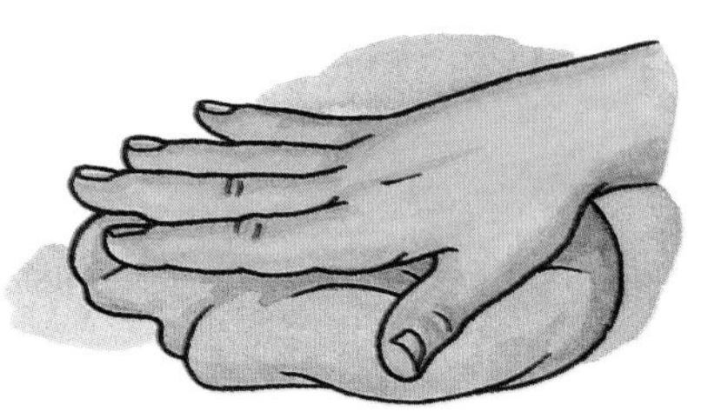

3. Want to make a nose or lips? Pinch the clay into shape by pressing it between your fingers and thumb.

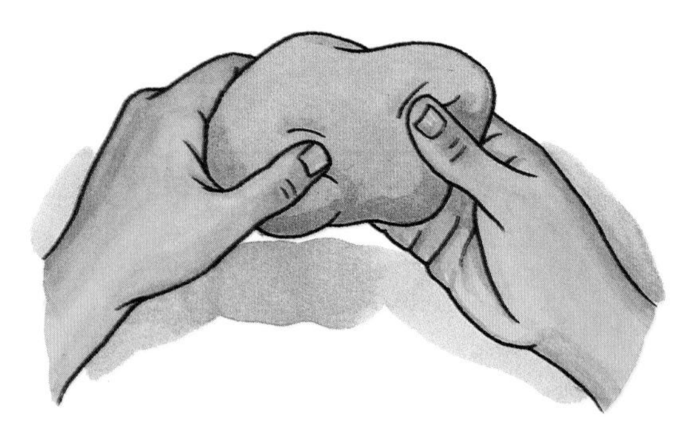

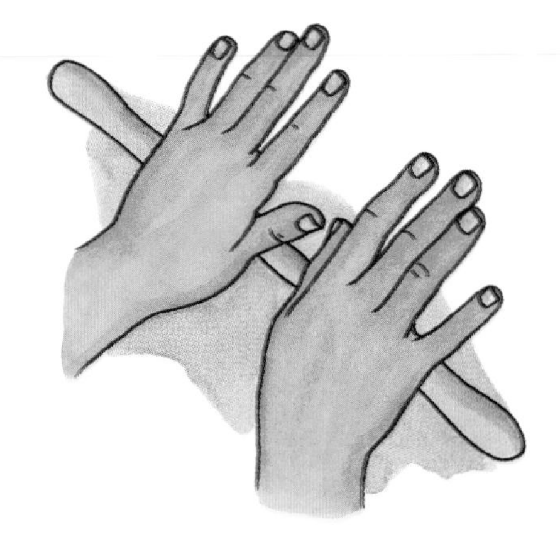

4. Want to make a tail? Use a coil. A coil is a ropelike piece of clay. To make one, roll the clay between the flat of your hand and the baking sheet. Roll the coil with both hands from the center to the ends until it is the thickness and length you want.

5. To draw a pattern on clay, use a toothpick or a pencil. Use cookie cutters to press shapes into the clay. Then press a comb, a pen, or other objects into the shapes to give them interesting textures.

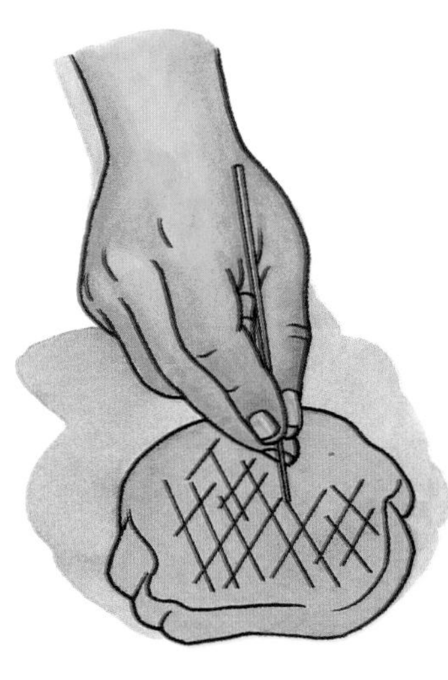

Show off your creations on a shelf. Or roll them up into a ball for more clay play later.

Getting Clay into Shape

You can use clay to mold almost anything—pots, people, puppies, you name it. How about starting with some funny animals?

You Will Need:

a baking sheet
clay
toothpicks
paper clips
beads
yarn
cloves or nuts

Make a Fish:

1. Roll clay into a ball. Place the clay on the baking sheet, and pat it with the palm of your hand. You should get a shape like a big biscuit.

2. Now pinch one end of the "biscuit" to form a tail.

3. Pinch the top and bottom to make fins, and pull the front into a mouth. Add tiny balls of clay for eyes.

4. To make overlapping scales, press a paper clip into the clay again and again.

Make a Snake:

1. On the baking sheet, roll a ball of clay into a coil. Roll one end of the coil thinner than the other end.

2. Use a toothpick to scratch eyes and a mouth on the thick end.

3. On the narrow end, scratch circles around the tail to make your snake a rattler.

Make a Prehistoric Parade:

1. Roll a ball of clay into a funny body shape. Make it short and chunky, or flat and long.

2. Shape other chunks of clay into a head and legs.

3. Use toothpicks, beads, yarn, cloves, and nuts to show eyes, scaly skin, big ears, spikes, or claws.

Clay animals are easy to pose. Give your creations funny poses and display them for fun.

The Great Sphinx

What has the body of a lion and the head of a man? A monster? No—a sphinx! A sphinx is a kind of statue sculpted in Egypt long ago. The Great Sphinx at Giza is the largest of these statues.

About 4,500 years ago, a gigantic limestone hill stood where the Great Sphinx is now. Stonecutters cut blocks from the limestone to build the Great Pyramid of Egypt's King Khufu. But the rock in the center of the hill was too crumbly to use for building.

On this leftover limestone, sculptors carved a rough face and body. To do this, they wedged picks in the stone and hit the picks with wooden hammers. Historians think that the face of the Great Sphinx was made to look like King Khafre, the son of Khufu.

Next, the sculptors covered the rough image with a kind of plaster. They could carve the plaster in greater detail than the coarse stone. Then artists painted the plaster to add even more detail. The Sphinx still wears bits of the red paint, but most of it wore away.

The Great Sphinx wears a royal headdress and lies near the pyramid of King Khafre.

The Master of Marble

Can you imagine a very young artist making statues so beautiful that centuries later people from around the world still travel to see them? This is what happened with Michelangelo Buonaroti, who grew up in Florence, Italy, in the late 1400's. At age 23, he completed his first *Pietà*—a larger-than-life marble statue of Mary and Jesus. The tools he used were like those the Egyptians used. But the stone he used was far better than crumbly limestone.

Marble is hard and long-lasting. The early Romans used marble for their temples and statues. By the 1500's, Italian sculptors were masters at working with marble. And Michelangelo was the best of them all.

Michelangelo's *Moses*

Michelangelo often chose his own blocks of marble at the quarries in Carrara, Italy. He searched for a block with even coloring and no tiny cracks. Then he planned the perfect sculpture for each block. Michelangelo often spoke of his work as freeing figures from the stone.

In this *Pietà,* Michelangelo carved the likeness of his own face on the figure of Joseph, the man holding Jesus.

First, he shaped a small model in wax. Next, he "roughed out" the figure in marble. To do this, he used a heavy hammer and metal points to knock away large chunks of stone. To hack away smaller chunks, Michelangelo used a lighter bronze hammer.

To bring out the figure's details, Michelangelo used chisels and rasps, or files. Finally, he polished the marble until it glowed. For this, he used pumice (PUHM ihs)—a kind of stone people use to smooth rough skin on their feet.

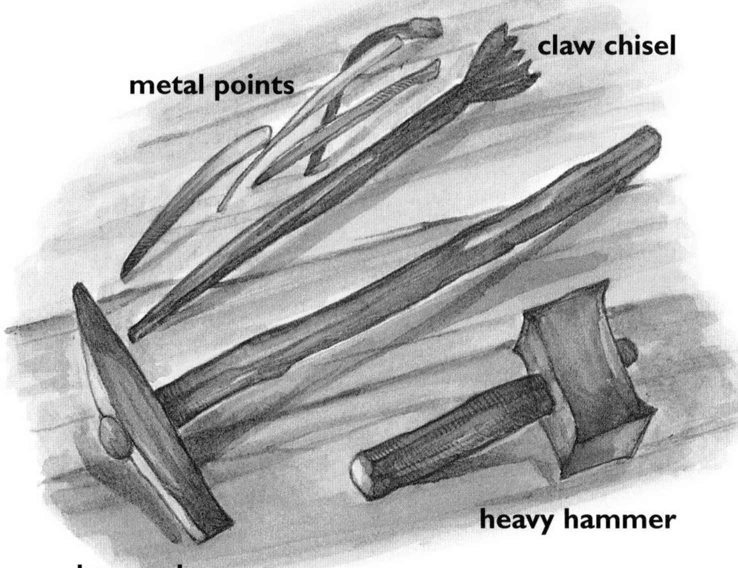

Wooden Wonders

raven

eagle

hawk

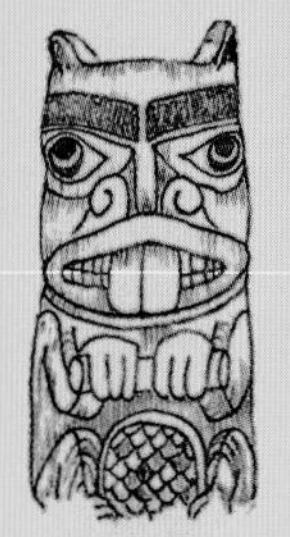
beaver

thunderbird

The early Nootka (NOOT kuh) people were Native Americans who lived on the Pacific Coast of North America near thick forests. The grandest trees in the forests were red cedars. They grew as tall as 20-story buildings and their wood outlasted most other woods. The Nootka used red cedar logs to carve their totem poles.

Totem poles stood in front of family houses. They served as a sort of address and a family history. The animal and human figures on the poles stood for great deeds in the family's past. The height of the pole and the detail of its carvings showed how rich the family was.

To make a totem pole, the carvers laid a red cedar trunk on its side. First, they peeled off the bark and the green wood beneath. Next, they used charcoal to etch designs into the log. Then they chopped out rough forms with a tool called an elbow adz (adz). Another type of adz is used like a chisel to smooth the rough forms. Finally, they cut out the details with a curved knife. The Nootka artists soaked the wood in hot water to keep it soft and workable while carving.

Other Native Americans besides the Nootka carved totem poles. The Tlingit people carved these totem poles.

Miniature Marvels

Foot soldiers march across the fields. On the hill behind the farmhouse, a hundred others advance toward the fighting. Meanwhile, the cavalry gallops in.

But this scene is not on a battlefield. It is in a museum. It was made by skilled model makers. They took great care to get the scene just right. They read maps and army reports of the battle, as well as diaries written by the soldiers and officers who were there. For instance, one soldier wrote that he had lost his boots near the farm. So the model makers made a tiny pair of boots and put them in the farmyard.

This scene is a model of the Battle of Waterloo fought in Belgium between the French and an army led by the British Duke of Wellington.

Everything in this miniature city in the Netherlands is 25 times smaller than life size.

Not all model makers work for museums. Some are architects. Architects make models of the full-sized buildings they design. These models, like the ones in the museum, are true to scale. For example, if a model of a building is made in a 1/10 scale, every wall and window in the full-sized building is exactly 10 times bigger than that same wall or window in the model. Even the bricks and doorknobs are true to scale.

The Shape of Space

For hundreds of years, sculptors have created art in two ways. They took away parts of material like stone or wood by carving it. Or they added to material, such as clay, and molded it.

In the 1900's, sculptors added space to their list of sculpting materials. They realized that everything and everyone takes up space. We see space around and inside objects. Modern sculptors use space to give it new meaning. But artists who sculpt space don't often carve or mold materials. They use materials in other ways.

An example of a twentieth-century "space" sculpture is *Linear Construction No. 4* by Russian-born Naum Gabo shown on the next page. He wove a complicated web on a simple frame. By doing so, Gabo created many planes, or surfaces, in space.

When you look at modern sculpture, you need imagination, too. If you had to describe this sculpture, what words would you use? What would you compare it to? After all, it has as many shapes as there are ways to look at it.

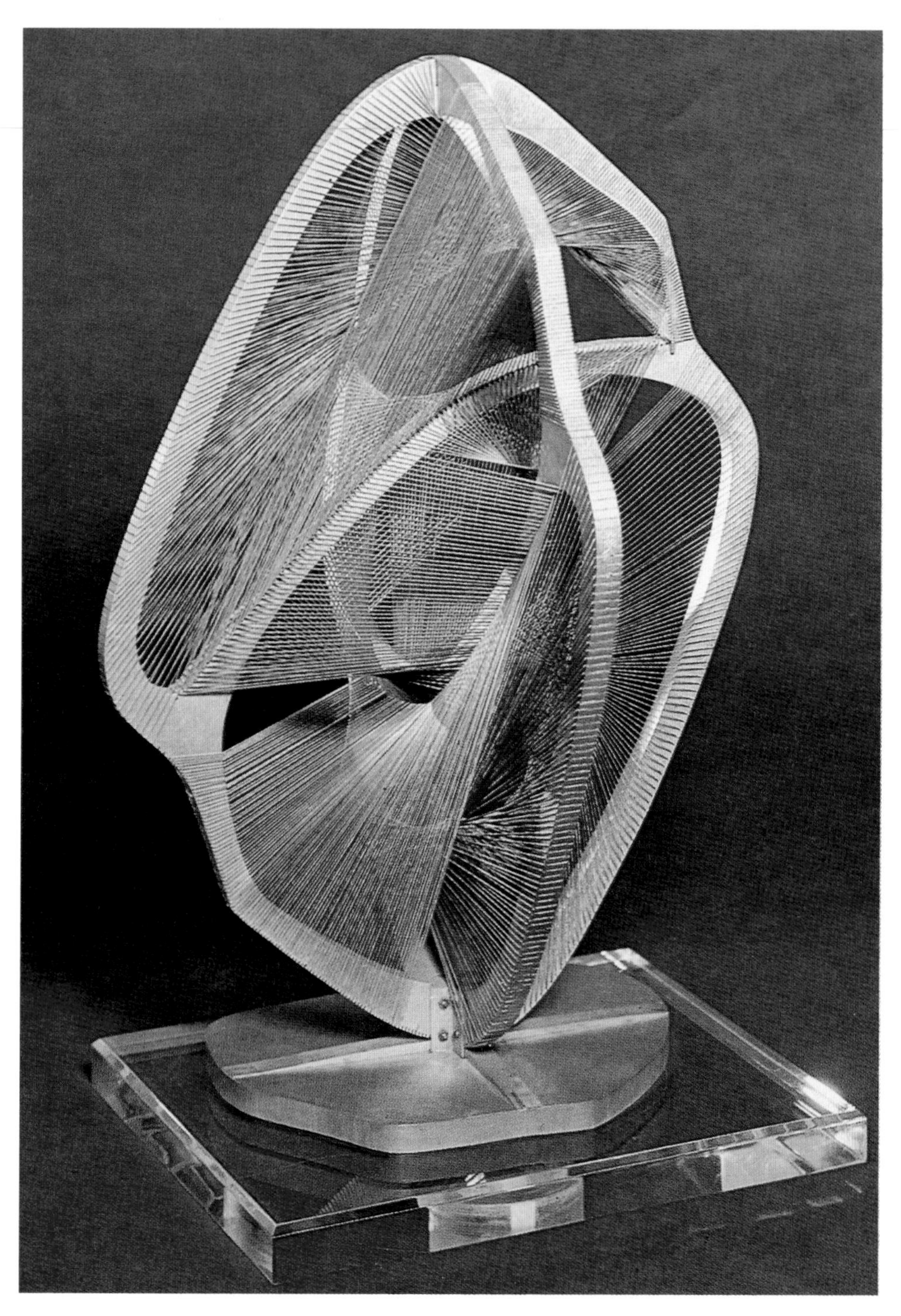

How would you describe *Linear Construction No. 4*, an aluminum and steel sculpture by Naum Gabo? How does it make you feel?

Assembling a Sculpture

TRY THIS! 2

You, too, can turn odds and ends into a work of art with a little glue, cardboard, and imagination. Hunt around your house. Find paper plates and cups, empty jars or cans, and bottle tops. Hunt through your toy box, too. Old puzzle pieces, play jewelry, old dolls, and action figures can add interest to your work of art.

After you've finished hunting, start arranging the pieces. Choose how you want to assemble them, for example, according to color or shape or theme.

You could cut a paper plate into a spiral and wrap it around a cup. Glue your pieces onto a piece of painted cardboard. If you like, paint the pieces, too. Then coat the entire work in white glue. Let it dry. Then display it for everyone to see!

Some modern sculptors don't really do much sculpting. Instead, they create **assemblages** (uh SEHM blihj ihz). In other words, they gather materials because they like their feel, their shape, or their color and put them together to make a sculpture. These assemblages may include odd things, such as old wheels or bits of plastic. Or they may be made of unusual but carefully chosen materials.

Sculptor Tony Cragg assembled *Red Bottle* and *Yellow Bottle* using objects he found—and his imagination! Compare the assemblages to the small bottles in front that inspired them!

An Owl Piñata

Many artists use **papier-mâché** (PAY puhr muh SHAY) to make sculptures. It can be made with newspaper mixed with paste. Papier-mâché is easy to press into shape when it is wet and becomes very hard when it dries. Find out for yourself about working with papier-mâché. Try making an owl **piñata** (peen YAH tuh). Piñatas are large hollow decorations from Mexico. They come in many shapes and are filled with candies and toys.

You Will Need:

white glue
warm water
a bowl
a large balloon
cooking oil
newspaper
wrapped candy and tiny toys
masking tape
scissors
orange and brown paper streamers
construction paper
a nail and hammer
string

What To Do:

1. Mix two parts glue with one part warm water in a bowl. Stir well.

2. Blow up the balloon, knot it, and rub it with the oil.

3. Tear the newspaper into strips about one inch wide. Dip the strips into the glue mixture. Cover the balloon, except for the knot, with a layer of strips going in one direction. Then cover the first layer with a second layer going in another direction. Apply three or four layers of this papier-mâché.

4. Let the balloon dry for 24 hours.

5. Burst the balloon at the knot and pull it free. Ask an adult to use the nail and hammer to make two small holes about one inch apart at the top of the piñata. Run a long piece of string through the holes and tie its ends.

6. Fill the hollow papier-mâché with candy and tiny toys. Close the hole where the knot was with masking tape.

7. To make feathers, cut a fringe on one side of the streamers. Put glue on the unfringed side of the streamers, and wind them around the owl. Draw eyes and a beak on construction paper. Cut them out, and glue them to the owl.

At parties in Mexico, children take turns batting at a hanging piñata. When it breaks open, the children scramble to get the treats that fall from it.

Auguste Rodin's Lifelike Sculptures

Sculptors often make statues of human bodies. After all, bodies have interesting shapes and different surfaces. Some of the most lifelike sculptures of human bodies are those by French sculptor Auguste Rodin (oh GOOST roh DAN).

Auguste Rodin

As a student, Rodin showed talent for only one thing—art. At age 16, he already wanted to be a sculptor. He applied to the best school of fine arts in Paris. In the 1800's, only students from this school were thought to be "real" artists.

Three times Rodin turned in a sculpture to qualify for the school, and he failed each time. At age 19, Rodin made up his mind to study on his own. He supported himself by designing plaster decorations for buildings.

Rodin greatly admired Michelangelo. Like Michelangelo, Rodin sculpted figures that seemed alive. He did not use the stiff poses that most sculptors of his day were using. Instead, he captured bodies in the act of movement.

Unlike Michelangelo, however, Rodin did not work in marble. He molded his figures in clay. Then, he made plaster casts of the clay statues. Skilled workers poured bronze into the casts to create the final work.

In 1877, a newspaper critic accused Rodin of cheating. The critic said Rodin had made a mold over a live model and then cast the mold in bronze. That is how lifelike Rodin's sculpture looked!

For years, art leaders in France had ignored Rodin's work. But the art critic's story suddenly made Rodin famous. People were very curious about his work. They wanted to see this famed sculptor and his work. By 1900, Rodin was world famous.

The Thinker sits outside the Rodin Museum in Paris.

Are You a Good Detective?

You Will Need:

a notebook
a pencil
walking shoes
a list of questions

Imagine walking through a great palace filled with beautiful treasures. That is exactly what art museums are! They are houses for artwork. Their paintings, photographs, crafts, and sculptures attract people from around the world. Some museums even house very old art, such as jewelry and pottery from Ancient Egypt.

Imagine someone replaced your favorite treasure with a copy. How might you help a detective find the real one?

What To Do:

1. Take a trip with an adult to an art museum.

2. At the museum, find a piece of art that has something that you like. For example, you might like animals, circles, a certain color, people eating, a party, flowers, or children. Then write the name of the art and the artist in your notebook. You are ready to begin your detective work!

3. Take a good look at your treasure. If someone stole it, how would you describe it to others so they could help find it?

Detective's Questions

What is the subject of this art?

How big is the art?

What colors are used?

What shapes do you see?

What are the tiniest details that you see?

Do you see brushstrokes or dabs or carved surfaces?

Does the art include people, trees, or flowers? If so, how many and what color?

If the art shows people, are they happy or sad? Are they laughing or talking? What do you think they are laughing about or discussing?

Are people in the art eating? What are they eating—breakfast, lunch, dinner, a special feast, or a snack?

How many animals are shown?

How many different colors can you see?

If the art includes children, what are they doing and how are they dressed?

Music to Your Ears

You can make music with your voice, your hands, and even your feet. Or you can use special sound makers called musical **instruments** (IHN struh muhnts). There are many kinds of musical instruments, but they make sounds in only a few ways. So you might think of each kind of instrument as a family. Every member of that family makes sounds in the same way.

One family has parts that you hit to make sounds. Another family has strings that you pluck or strum. Two families have tubes you blow into. And a few instruments belong to families that make sounds in yet other ways.

Music Around the World

Good times everywhere are even better with music. But the sound of music can be different from place to place. Why? Because **orchestras** (AWR kuhs truhs) and bands in different parts of the world play different kinds of instruments.

For example, in North America and Western Europe, many people like big bands with **brass** instruments. Also, many young people listen to rock groups with electric guitars and **synthesizers** (SIHN thuh SY zuhrz).

In Mexico, people of all ages enjoy mariachi (mahr ee AH chee) bands with non-electric guitars and accordions (uh KAWR dee uhnz)—keyboard instruments that you squeeze to make sounds. Farther south in Ecuador, Inca musicians play **panpipes** and **marimbas** (muh RIHM buhz).

In China, musical groups play bells, drums, gongs, flutes, and stringed instruments called the quin (chihn) and the pipa (PY pah). In Japan, special musical groups called gagaku (guh GAH koo) also play bells, drums, gongs, flutes, and their own kinds of ancient stringed instruments. In Indonesia, the popular **gamelan** (GAH muh LAN) orchestra includes many instruments that are played by striking them.

A Gamelan orchestra of Indonesia includes double-ended drums, xylophones, and flutes.

Singing and Speaking

When you sing, you are a musical instrument. When you speak, you are not. Singing and speaking are different, even though you make the sounds in similar ways.

You sing and speak by making your **vocal cords** vibrate, or move back and forth. These cords are a pair of small, stretchy bands in your throat.

When you are not singing or speaking, your vocal cords relax. Your breath

This South African group sings in Zulu and English.

goes in and out between the vocal cords without making them vibrate.

When you begin to speak, small muscles in your throat pull the vocal cords tight. The air you breathe out makes the vocal cords vibrate. This vibration produces sounds. Your tongue and lips make the sounds into words.

When you sing, your vocal cords vibrate in the same way, but at a different speed. To sing high, your vocal cords tighten. This makes them vibrate faster. To sing low, your vocal cords loosen. This slows the vibrations. So your vocal cords vibrate at exactly the right speed for each sound. Your voice is making music!

Top view of voice box

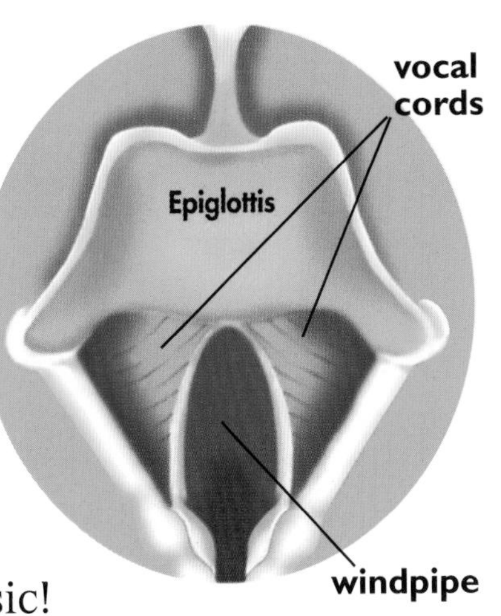

Boom! Bong! Bam!

Tap a pencil against a box. It doesn't play a tune, but it does make a sound. One family of instruments makes sounds in the same way—you use something to hit or strike them. The instruments in this family are called **percussion** (puhr KUH shuhn) instruments. The word *percussion* means "striking."

Drums, gongs, cymbals (SIHM buhls), and bells are percussion instruments. Musicians hit gongs with sticks that look like small hammers. Musicians hit two cymbals together. And they shake bells so that the clappers hit the insides of the bells.

Most drums, such as the Irish bodhran (BOH rawn) and African long drums, make only one sound. They are used to set the beat in a song. Each has a thin piece of animal skin or plastic called the drumhead, stretched over a hollow body. When you strike

bodhran

When you strike the drumhead, the air inside the drum vibrates.

the drumhead, the air inside the drum bounces around, or vibrates. This makes the sound stronger. So instead of a light tapping, you hear a loud *rat-tat-tat* or even a *boom-boom-boom.*

Some drums, such as **timpani** (TIHM puh nee), or kettle drums, can make several different sounds. The drumheads are tightened to make high sounds and loosened to make lower sounds.

tom-tom drum

Other percussion instruments that play tunes are the xylophone (ZY luh fohn) and marimba. Each has bars of different lengths that make different sounds when you hit them. The short bars vibrate faster and make higher sounds than the long bars.

marimba

Singing Strings

Can you make a string sing? When you play an instrument from the string family, that's exactly what you do. Rubbing or plucking the **strings** makes them produce sounds.

To play a **violin** (vy uh LIHN), you stroke its strings with a bow (boh). A bow is a wooden stick with horsehair stretched from one end to the other. Stroking the strings makes them vibrate, or "sing."

The strings of the violin are stretched over a thin wooden part called a bridge. As the strings vibrate, they make the bridge vibrate. The vibrating bridge sends sound bouncing around inside the violin. All these vibrations produce the music you hear. You can make the sounds higher or lower by pressing down on the violin strings in different places. Pressing a string

Some children begin playing violins at a young age.

These young women play a traditional Finnish harp called the *kantele*.

changes the length of the part that vibrates. The shorter the vibrating part, the faster it moves and the higher the note sounds.

Some stringed instruments are played without a bow. The sitar (sih TAHR), for instance, is played with a wire pick worn on the musician's right index finger. The musician plucks the strings to play a tune. A harp is played by plucking the strings with your fingers.

Wind Instruments

This flute is called a concert flute and is made of metal.

Have you ever whistled a happy tune? Many instruments make music the same way you do when you whistle—by using a stream of air. These instruments belong to the wind family. They are all played with "wind"—your breath.

Some wind instruments are called **woodwinds**, because many of them were once made of wood. These include flutes and clarinets.

A concert flute has a mouthpiece with a small hole on the top. When you blow across the hole, the air inside the flute vibrates. The vibrations inside the tube create sound waves, and these sound waves make the music.

To make or play notes, you press keys that open "windows" for the air. If you open the holes close to the mouthpiece, the vibrations travel a short distance to reach an opening. So the air forms short sound waves—and high notes. If you open holes farther down the tube, the vibrations travel farther. This forms longer sound waves—and lower notes.

Some flutes are blown from the end instead of the side. To play a Japanese bamboo flute called a shakuhachi (SHAH koo HA chee), you cover one of its ends with your chin and blow into a notch on the top of the flute. To make or play different notes, you cover or uncover the holes along the flute with your fingers and thumb.

This man is playing a Japanese bamboo flute called the shakuhachi.

Brass instruments are part of the wind family of instruments. Where does the loud, sharp sound of a trumpet come from? It starts with you, the musician.

When you blow into a trumpet, you vibrate your lips against the cup-shaped mouthpiece. This makes the air in the trumpet vibrate and create a sound. Try changing the shape of your lips. This makes the air vibrate faster to make a high note or slower to make a low note.

This boy must blow hard to play the trumpet.

This baritone, a popular type of tuba, has very long tubes. It produces longer sound waves and lower notes than a trumpet.

You can also change the sound by making the vibrating air travel farther. A trumpet has several loops of tube. When you press a button, you open a valve (valv), or doorway, in a loop. When vibrations travel through extra loops, they make a lower sound.

The slide trombone has tubes but no valves. To make high or low notes, you slide a U-shaped tube in and out. The shorter you make the tube, the shorter the sound wave and the higher the note.

Keyboards

Have you ever made music by pressing keys? If you play an instrument from the keyboard family, you have. The most popular keyboard instruments are the piano, harpsichord, and pipe organ.

In a piano, small hammers hitting the wire strings make the sounds you hear. The strings are different sizes. Long, thick strings that vibrate slowly make the low sounds. And short, thin strings that vibrate very quickly make the high sounds.

When you press down a piano key, two things happen. A small cushion swings out of the way so the strings for that key can vibrate. At the same time, the key pushes a lever. This lever swings the hammer against the strings.

Electronic Music

Some instruments have no strings, no tubes, and no hammers. These instruments use an electric current to produce music.

A synthesizer (SIHN thuh SY zuhr) is an electric keyboard that can make sounds like almost any instrument. The music made by a synthesizer may sound like a single flute or a room full of bells or a giant duck—or all of these things together. It can also create sounds unlike those of any other instruments.

Let's Make Music

The simple instruments on these pages have lots of "relatives." Can you name the family to which each belongs?

You Will Need:

a book
a plastic cup
a rubber band

Rubber-band strummer

This two-stringed instrument is like the Kutyapi. The Kutyapi has been played in the Philippines for hundreds of years. What other instruments is this like?

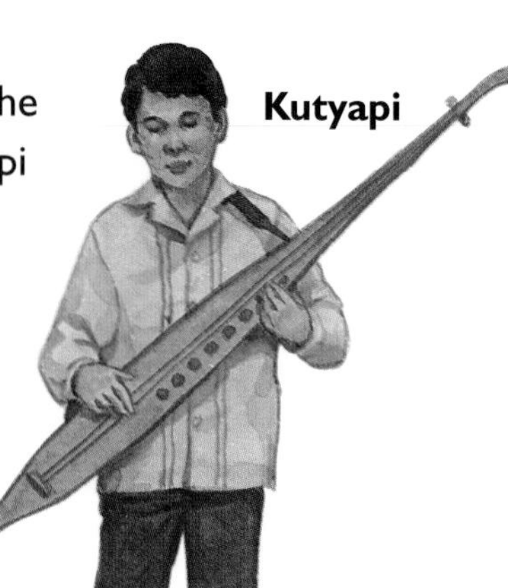

What To Do:

1. Place the cup—open end up—on the book. Stretch the rubber band around the length of the book and over the cup.

2. Strum the part of the rubber band across the top of the cup. Then strum the rubber band on each side of the cup. Do you hear three different sounds?

3. To change the sounds, move the cup. The shorter and tighter you make one part of the rubber band, the higher the sound it makes.

4. When you find notes that sound good together, try strumming a three-note **melody**.

Coffee-can bongos

Bongos are similar to the tabla (TAH blah), an instrument played in India. The tabla sometimes includes two drums, one played with the right hand and the other with the left hand. What other kinds of drums do you know?

tabla

You Will Need:

2 coffee cans—
I large, I small
plastic lids for cans
masking tape

What To Do:

1. Snap the lids onto the cans. Then turn the cans upside down on a table.

2. Have a friend hold the cans while you tape them together. Wind two or three layers of tape around the cans. Then turn the cans right side up. If you want to, you can decorate the tape with stars or another design.

3. To play the bongos, sit on a chair or on the floor and hold them between your knees. Tap each drum with your fingertips. The smaller drum will make a higher sound than the larger one.

Blow your horn! Toot a flute!

Bottle trombone

Would you like to play the trombone? If so, you don't need to buy or borrow an expensive instrument. You can make your own bottle trombone!

You Will Need:

a bottle
a drinking straw
water

trombone

What To Do:

1. Find a bottle that is almost as long as or longer than your straw. Clean the bottle, and fill it three-quarters full with water.

2. Stick the straw into the water. Holding the straw in one hand and the bottle in the other, blow across the top of the straw.

3. Move the bottle up and down as you blow. When most of the straw is in the water, only a short part of the tube is filled with vibrating air. Blowing the "trombone" makes a high sound. When most of the straw is out of the water, the air-filled part is longer and the sound is lower.

bottle trombones

Cardboard flute

Asian Indians play an instrument called a *bansuri*. The bansuri is a simple flute made from bamboo. It uses no keys and requires careful fingering on its six or seven holes. Make your own cardboard flute and enjoy!

bansuri

You Will Need:

- a cardboard paper towel tube
- wax paper
- a pencil
- a rubber band
- scissors

What To Do:

1. Use a pencil to poke holes along one side of a cardboard tube.
2. Cover one end of the tube with a piece of wax paper.
3. Hold the wax paper in place with a rubber band as shown.

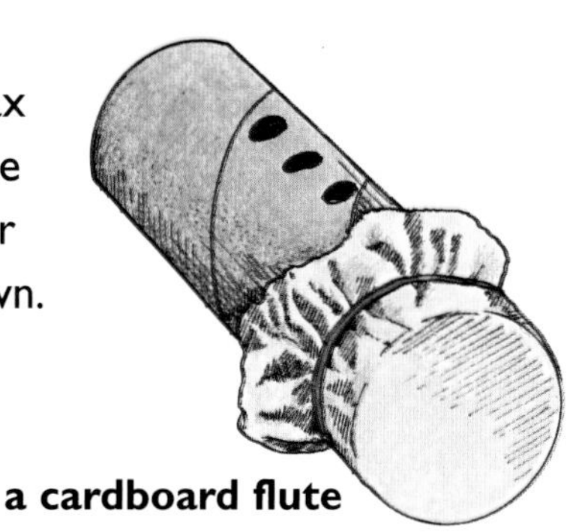

a cardboard flute

Hum into the uncovered end of the tube as you move your fingers over the holes. Toot, toot! You're playing a tune on your own flute.

The Basic Ingredients of Music

To make a cake, a baker uses basic ingredients like flour, sugar, and oil. To make music, a **composer**—a person who makes up music—uses basic ingredients too. They are **tone**, **rhythm** (RIH thuhm), melody, and **harmony**.

Tone is the difference in pitch between two notes. Pitch is the highness or lowness of a note's sound. Notes are the building blocks of a piece of music.

Different notes are held for different lengths of time. Some notes last a long time just like some sounds do. Think of the slow *swish-swish* of windshield wipers. Other notes last a short time—like the rapid raindrops in a storm. A composer mixes slow and quick notes to create rhythm.

Melody is the part of music that people hum. To make a melody, a composer mixes tones and rhythms. Short pieces of music, such as songs, have only one melody. Long pieces, such as

symphonies (SIHM fuh neez), have several melodies.

A composer creates harmony by sounding three or more notes together. Most music in Western countries is based on the idea of harmony.

Prokofiev, the Children's Composer

Imagine composing songs for a play at age 9. Sergei Prokofiev (praw KAW fyehf) did just that. Prokofiev's play, *The Giant*, included marches and waltzes. It also told of an outlaw giant who became a king.

Sergei Prokofiev

Prokofiev was born in 1891 in Ukraine, a country in Europe. (At that time, Ukraine was part of Russia.) Like most children, Sergei enjoyed fairy tales. But he considered them amusing rather than magical.

Prokofiev did not like popular tunes. He preferred music that surprised people and made them smile. He developed his talent for writing such music at the Conservatory, a music school in St. Petersburg, Russia.

In 1917, there was a revolution in Russia. A Communist government took over. The Communist rulers tried to control the arts as well as the government. So Prokofiev left Russia for the United States in 1918.

Within five years, orchestras in the United States and Europe were performing Prokofiev's music. In 1927, the Communists welcomed Prokofiev's performances to the Soviet Union, the new name for Russia. Nine years later,

Peter and the Wolf helps children learn about the sounds of different instruments.

Prokofiev, his wife, and their two sons moved to the Soviet Union and settled in Moscow.

Soon after, Prokofiev wrote *Peter and the Wolf* for the Moscow Children's Musical Theater. He gave each character its own special music. Violins play when Peter takes the stage. Flutes announce the presence of a bird. An oboe speaks for a duck, and a French horn warns that the wolf is near.

Peter and the Wolf has been loved by children for years. It also helps children recognize the sounds of different instruments.

Clap and Rest

A composer uses notes—the written signs that show the length and the highness or lowness of sound—to write music on paper just as an author uses letters to write a story. Composers use different kinds of notes to tell musicians how long to play each sound.

This note, for example, is a quick note, like a clap of your hands or saying "oh:"

These are notes in order from shortest to longest sound:

Sometimes the composer wants the music to stop for a few beats. Composers show this by using symbols called rests.

These are three kinds of rests:

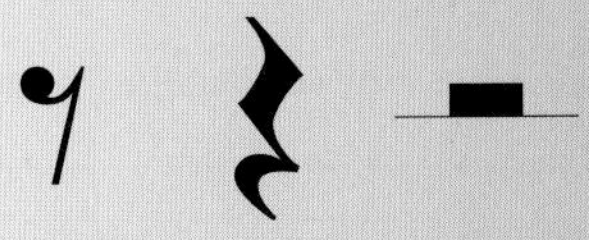

This rest means to pause for just a short moment:

This rest means to pause a little longer:

This rest means to stop for even longer:

How do you know how high or low to sing or play a note? A composer arranges them on a group of five or ten lines called a staff. High notes go on the upper lines. Low notes go on the lower lines.

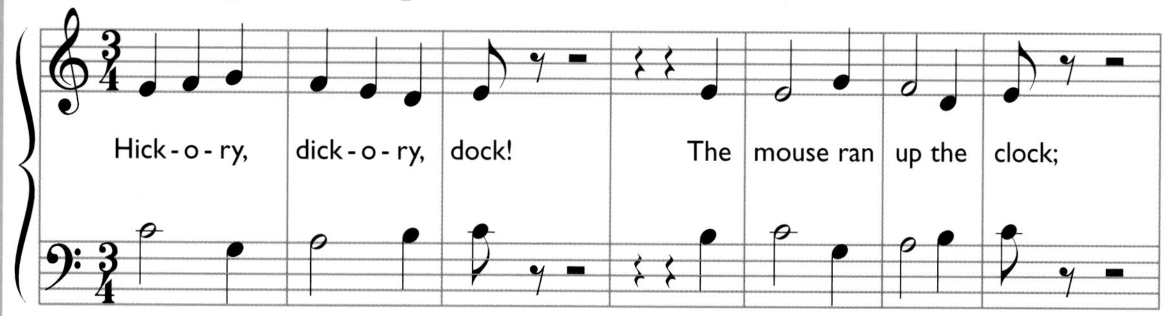

Can you identify the notes and rests in this line from a song? Which are held for the longest time? Which are quick sounds or pauses?

Musical Scales Around the World

A musical scale is a set of notes arranged from the lowest pitch to the highest. Western composers—those from America, Europe, and Australia—call the notes in their scale A, B, C, D, E, F, and G. The distance between a note and the next highest note by the same name is called an octave (AHK tihv).

An octave also includes sharps—half tones above notes—and flats—half tones below notes. The distance between a note and its sharp or a note and its flat is called a half step. The letter notes and half steps add up to a total of 12 full steps in the Western scale.

Music from countries in the eastern part of the world, such as China, India, and Saudi Arabia, sounds different from Western music, because Asian music has more kinds of notes than Western music has. For example, the Arab scale has 17 steps in each octave. The Indian scale has even more—22 steps.

The black keys on a piano keyboard play sharps and flats. The white keys play the full steps in the scale.

All Together Now

Imagine yourself in a big hall where a large orchestra (AWR kuhs truh) is preparing to play. The musicians are tuning up their instruments. It sounds noisy. Why? The instruments are not in harmony yet.

Soon, the performance begins. Each family of instruments has a special job. Some instruments—the strings, brass, or

All the players in an orchestra must watch the conductor as well as their music.

woodwinds—play the melody. Others, such as drums, make the beat or the rhythm. Different instruments add different tones. The woodwinds sound soft and light, while the brass instruments provide a strong background. All the instruments play in harmony. In other words, they sound good together.

During the concert, the musicians watch the conductor's signals. The conductor holds a small stick called a baton in the right hand. The baton tells the musicians when to play slow and when to play fast.

With the left hand, the conductor points to different parts of the orchestra. This signals them that it is time for them to play. The left hand also tells the musicians whether to play soft or loud.

Some conductors even use facial (FAY shuhl) expressions. They make themselves look happy, or sad, or angry. These facial expressions show the musicians how their music should make listeners feel.

A conductor uses the baton in his right hand to tell the orchestra how fast or slow to play. With the left hand, he signals to parts of the orchestra to play.

Music of the People

Once a jolly swagman camped
beside a billabong,
Under the shade of a coolibah tree,
And he sang as he sat and waited
while his billy boiled,
"Who'll come a-waltzing Matilda with me?"

These are words from "Waltzing Matilda," an Australian ballad, or song that tells a story. Ballads are one kind of folk music. Folk music includes all the traditional songs of a country or group of people.

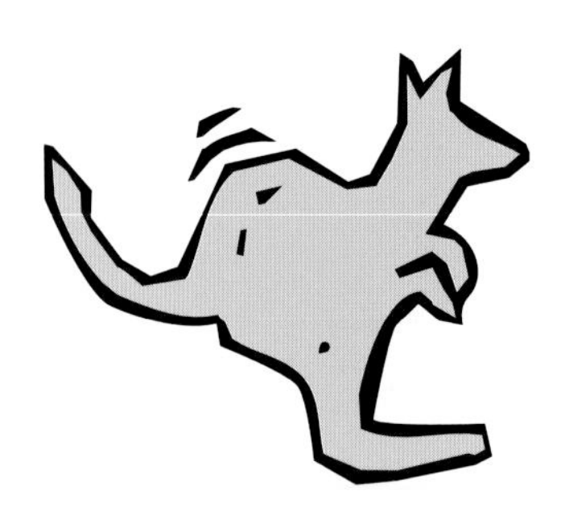

People learn folk songs by listening. They pass the song from person to person, from place to place, and from parents to children. Often the melody and words develop over many years. So, most of the time, nobody knows who made up a folk song.

Some songs that are written by composers become folk songs, too. If many people in a country like a song and sing it often, they think of it as theirs. It says something about their people and their country.

People in Australia think of "Waltzing Matilda" as their song. And when people around the world hear the song, they think of Australians. So although the composer is known—his name is "Banjo" Paterson—"Waltzing Matilda" is certainly a folk song, a song of the people.

KNOW It All!

In Australian slang, *Waltzing Matilda* means "tramping the roads." A *swagman* is a tramp, a *billabong* is a pond, a *coolibah* is a eucalyptus tree, and a *billy* is a small can.

The Power of Music

This is the legend of The Pied Piper. *It is the story of a piper who came to the town of Hamelin and bewitched the town's rats—and later its children—by playing a haunting melody on his pipe.*

Long ago, thousands of rats invaded the German town of Hamelin. The rats were everywhere. They even swarmed into the houses. People could not move without touching a rat. Neither cats nor traps could destroy the swarm of rats.

One Friday, a piper wearing a many-colored cloak came to town. "I can rid your town of rats," the piper told the mayor.

"Then I will pay you one coin a head," the mayor said.

As soon as the moon rose, the stranger started playing a haunting tune. Rats ran out of all the houses into the town square. The piper played a lively tune and led the rats to the nearby Weser River. The rats rushed to the water and jumped right in.

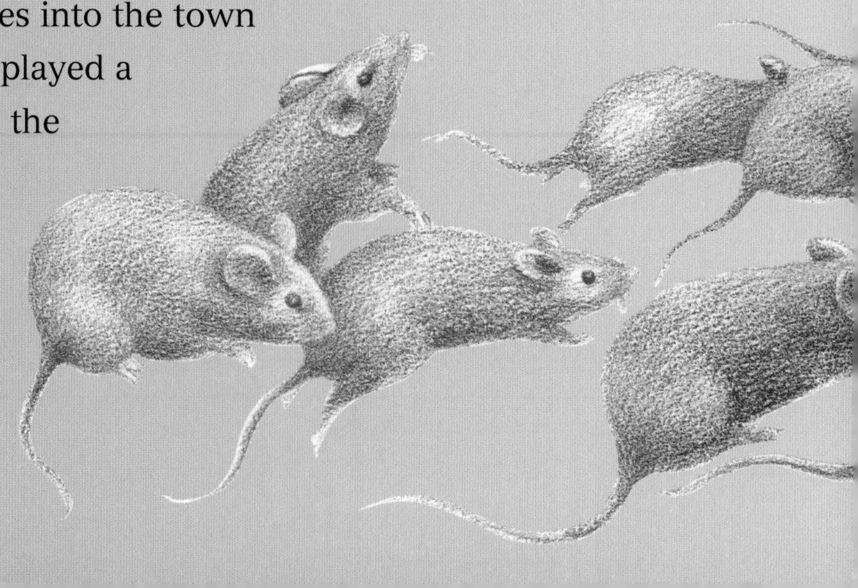

"Pay me," the piper said to the mayor on Saturday morning."Nine hundred and ninety thousand, nine hundred and ninety nine rats drowned in the river. You owe me one coin a head."

"Let us count the heads first," the mayor said.

"If you want the heads," the piper cried, "fetch them from the river."

"By rights, we can refuse to pay you anything," the mayor answered.

"If you do not pay me, your children will," said the piper.

"Collect from our children?" the townspeople jeered. "How cleverly the mayor has tricked the piper!"

On Sunday, after the townspeople returned from church, they looked all around for their sons and

daughters. “Where can they be?” the people asked.

In all of Hamelin, only one lame boy remained. “The piper played a haunting tune, and the children followed him out of town,” the boy told their parents. “That nearby hill opened wide, and they marched right in. By the time I reached the hill, the opening had closed.”

The parents ran out of town with axes and hammers. They tried but failed to open up the hill that had swallowed their children. Most miserable of all was the mayor. He had lost three boys and two girls.

“The mayor should have paid the piper,” the townspeople moaned. “How could we think he was clever? He is the biggest fool of us all!”

Theater

We find our seats in the theater. The lights dim, the audience hushes, and the curtains draw slowly back. It's showtime!

The show might be a play, a dance, a musical comedy, or any of the other kinds of stories performed on stage. It can make us laugh, surprise us, or even make us cry.

No one knows for sure how the kinds of shows we see at the theater began. But nearly every country has had some form of theater. Most likely, theater began with people's love of storytelling. Early hunters surely gathered around the evening fire and told about the day's adventures. Later these stories probably grew into plays, songs, and dances.

Theater Around the World

People all around the world love going to the **theater**. Most big cities have many theater buildings. To many people, "American theater" means whatever is playing in New York City's Broadway district. London's Royal Ballet and Royal National Theatre feature some of the world's best dancers, directors, and actors. And the Comédie-Française in Paris, France, is one of the world's oldest theaters still in use.

William Shakespeare, a great English playwright, based many of his plays on old Greek plays and stories.

Stories in traditional Indian theater are like long poems.

All these cities offer Western theater—a style of storytelling that began in early Greece. Stories of comedy and tragedy came from the ancient Greeks. Comedies are funny. Tragedies are sad. Western theater also followed the Greek custom of dividing stories into parts called acts.

Theater from the eastern part of the world, such as from Asia, is very different and tells stories in other ways.

Theater in India goes back about 2,000 years. Stories told in Indian theaters are like long poems. And all Indian plays have happy endings.

KNOW It All!

What is a person who writes plays called? A playwright. The word *wright* means "someone who works or makes things," and a playwright makes plays.

Chinese theater is about 800 years old. China's most popular form of play today is Peking **opera** (AH puh ruh). Its plays are based on Chinese stories, history, and folklore. Actors may change or make up their lines as they go along.

The stage in Peking opera looks bare compared to Western stages. Often special props—the objects that the actors use onstage—are the only clues to where a play takes place. For example, if an actor carries a whip, the audience knows he is outdoors riding a horse.

Also, the actors are never the only ones onstage. Musicians and prop people stay

A Peking opera company performs *The Monkey King* at the Beijing Opera.

Kabuki began in the 1600's.

on the stage during the performance, but the actors and audience pretend they are invisible.

In Japan, the oldest form of drama is the *noh* play. It includes drama, dance, song, and choruses—groups of actors speaking lines together. Men play both male and female parts. The actors with female roles wear masks. Unlike the plays of Peking Opera, every detail in a noh play is traditional—and never changed.

The most popular kind of theater in Japan today is *Kabuki* (kah BOO kee). Female dancers acted out the earliest Kabuki plays. But later on, men played all the parts. Kabuki plays are something like noh plays, but Kabuki theater has richer scenery and more exciting stories.

Welcome to La Scala

What does a world-famous theater look like? To find out, let's go to Milan, Italy, to visit La Scala, where some of the most famous operas were first performed. It is a theater built for a type of play called **opera**. In Western opera, the actors sing their lines.

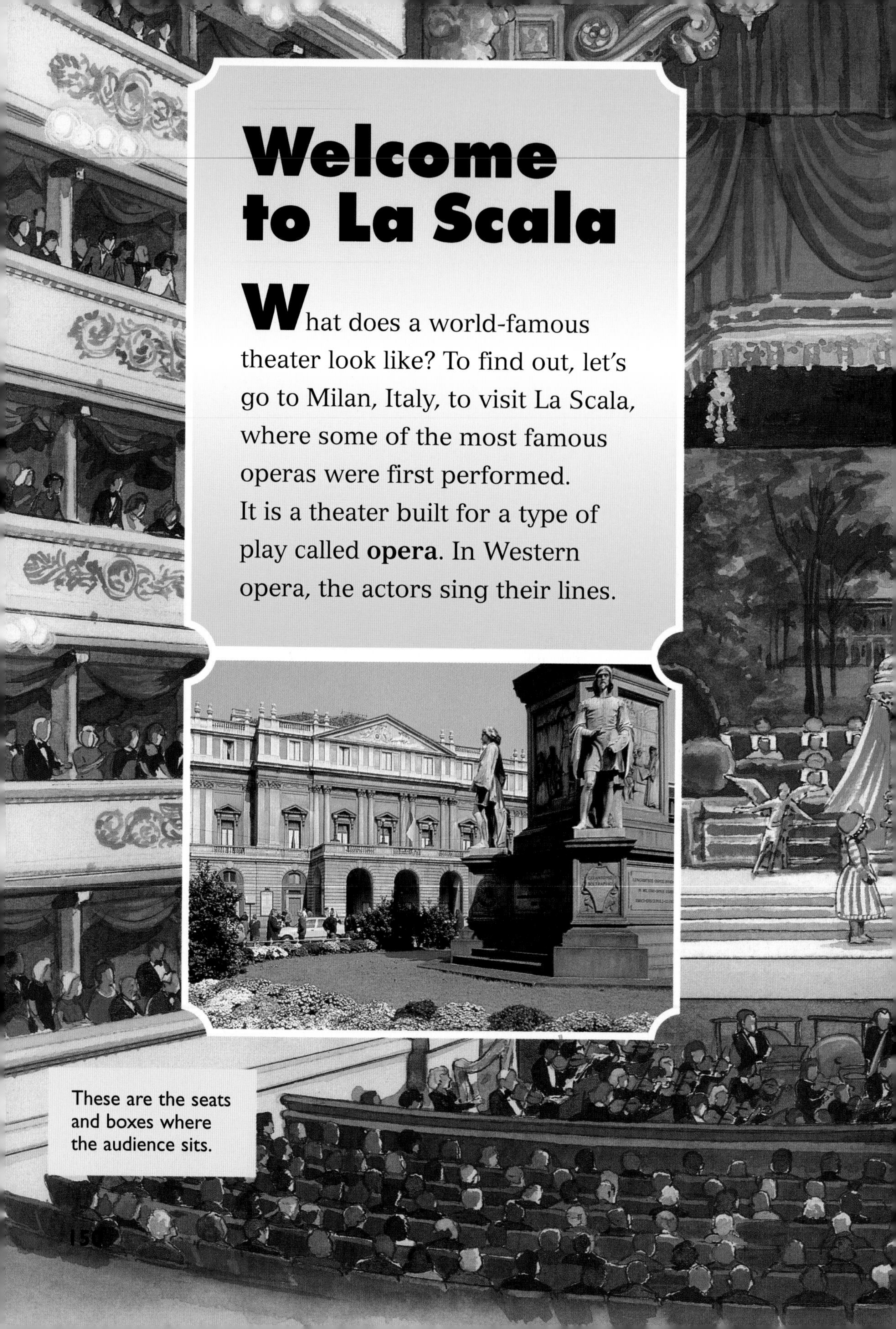

These are the seats and boxes where the audience sits.

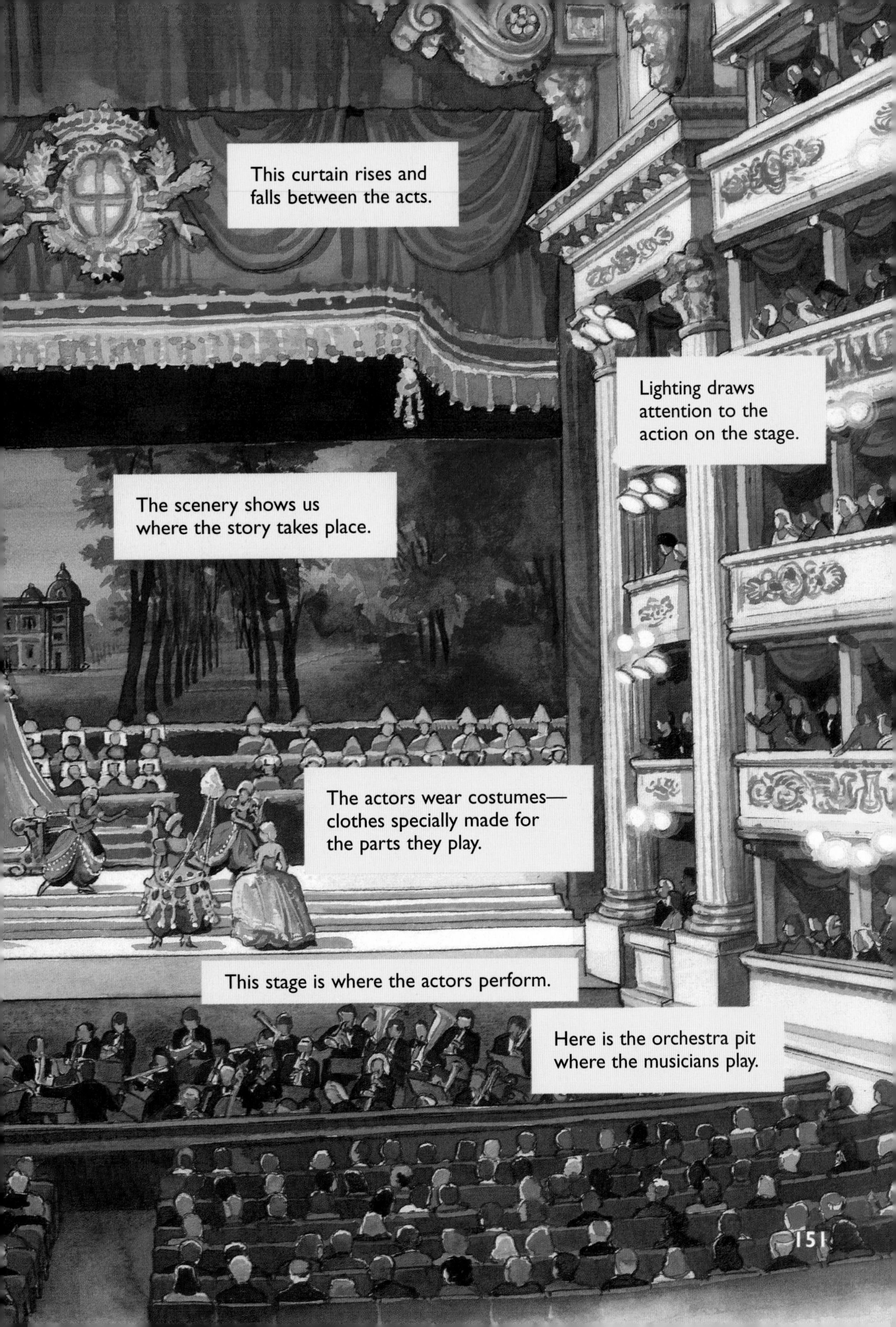
This curtain rises and falls between the acts.
Lighting draws attention to the action on the stage.
The scenery shows us where the story takes place.
The actors wear costumes—clothes specially made for the parts they play.
This stage is where the actors perform.
Here is the orchestra pit where the musicians play.

How Do You Put on a Play?

What happens at theaters before the opening of a play? The cast has lots to do as it prepares for its big night.

The actors memorize their lines. They also memorize as many lines of the other characters as possible. This helps them to recognize their cues. Cues are the last words spoken by another character before an actor says his or her line.

At the first rehearsal, the director blocks, or plans every

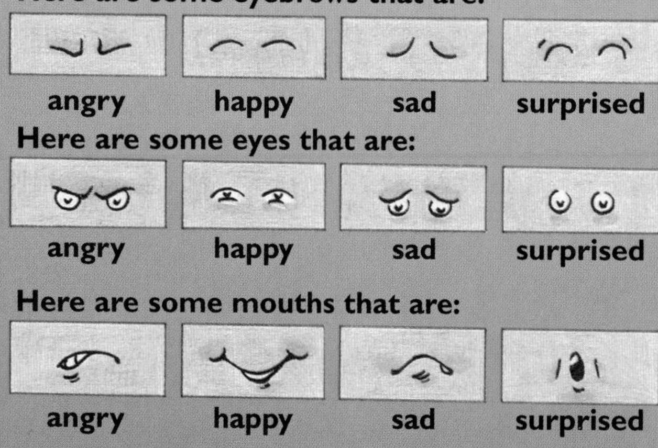

At rehearsals, the director suggests ways actors can show feelings. For example, if a character feels surprise, the actor might open his or her eyes and mouth wide. If a character feels anger, the actor might shake a fist or clench his or her jaw.

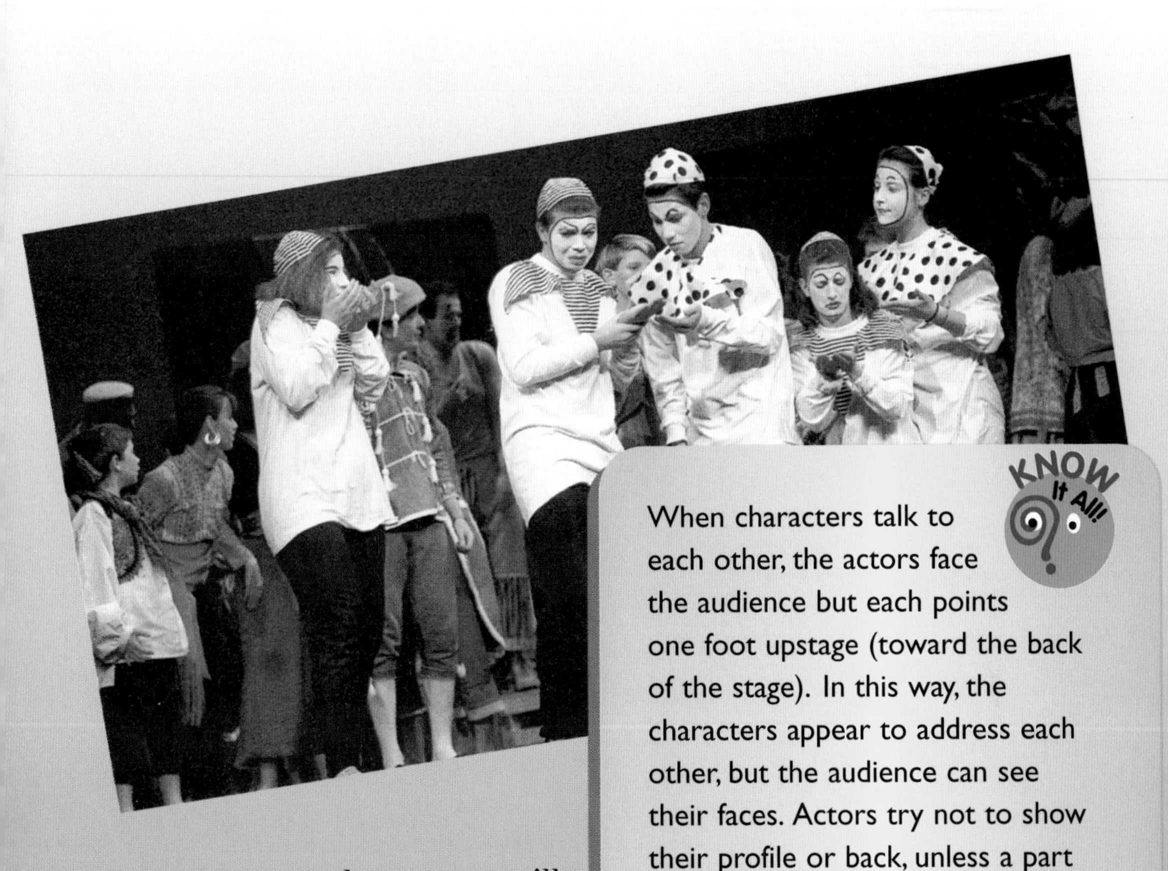

movement the actors will make onstage. The director also shows the actors how to move and where to stand.

KNOW It All!

When characters talk to each other, the actors face the audience but each points one foot upstage (toward the back of the stage). In this way, the characters appear to address each other, but the audience can see their faces. Actors try not to show their profile or back, unless a part requires it, for example, a werewolf who changes makeup onstage.

At dress rehearsal, or the last day of practice, the stagehands set up all the scenery. The actors put on their makeup and costumes. The play manager gets programs, tickets, and everything else ready for opening night.

On opening night, all the actors practice their lines without scripts. Then they go onstage and perform for the audience.

Stage an African Folktale

Here's a play made from a folk tale of the Hausa (HOW sah) people in Africa. Sadiki (sah DEE kee) is a young Hausa man who was kidnapped by enemies and forced to do chores in their village. He manages to escape with his only possessions—a goat, a leopard, and a yam.

Grab a friend or two and pick characters. Take turns reading the lines of the play. On the pages following the script are instructions for how to make costumes.

Cast of Characters:
Sadiki, Yam, Goat, Leopard

Setting: *A river flows center stage. A jungle grows on either bank. To the left, a canoe rests near a large rock.*

Time: *Before breakfast*

(The yam rolls to the edge of the river. The leopard leaps onstage followed by Sadiki. The goat ambles in.)

Sadiki: *(resting on the rock and looking nervous)* The sun is up. Soon the villagers will be looking for me.

Goat: But Boss, now you are free and ready to start anew.

Yam: With a yam, a goat, and a leopard. What more could you ask, Boss?

Goat: We need a better head start on the villagers who are after us. Let's board this canoe and put the river between us and them.

Goat: *(studying the canoe)* This small canoe can carry only two of us.

Yam: *(fearfully)*
Boss must paddle, so only one of us can go with him.

Sadiki: I shall simply cross the river several times. Will you be first to cross, Yam?

Goat: Oh no, Boss! Then I will be left alone with the leopard, and she will surely eat me.

Sadiki: So the leopard should go first.

Yam: Oh, no, Boss. Then I will be left alone with the goat, and he will surely eat me.

Sadiki: So the goat goes first.

(Sadiki and the goat cross the river.)

Yam: *(eyeing the leopard)*
How hungry are you?

Leopard: *(disdainfully)*
Silly Yam! Vegetables are for goats.

(Sadiki returns.)

Sadiki: Your turn, Yam.

Yam: *(hysterical)* Oh, no, Boss! When you return for the leopard, I will be alone with the goat on the other side of the river, and he will eat me.

Sadiki: *(as they cross the river)* Don't worry, Yam. I have a plan.

Goat: *(licking his chops)* Good choice, Boss.

Sadiki: You sly goat, get in the canoe.

(Sadiki and the goat return to the left bank. Sadiki leads the goat out of the canoe.)

Leopard: Yum, here comes my lunch.

Sadiki: Your turn to get in the boat, Leopard.

(The leopard joins the yam on the other side of the river as Sadiki returns a fourth time for the goat.)

Goat: So Boss figured out how to keep you safe and me hungry.

Yam: *(smugly)* Planning keeps people the masters and us their servants.

Sadiki Costume

Follow these directions to make a costume for the Sadiki character in the play you just read.

You Will Need:

an extra large T-shirt
straight pins
an old white sheet (ask a grown-up)
scissors
a needle
thread
markers
a ruler

What To Do:

1. Fold the sheet in half. Pin the T-shirt on the sheet with the neck and sleeves at the fold. Cut the sheet around the shirt. Do not cut the fold at the top of the sheet.

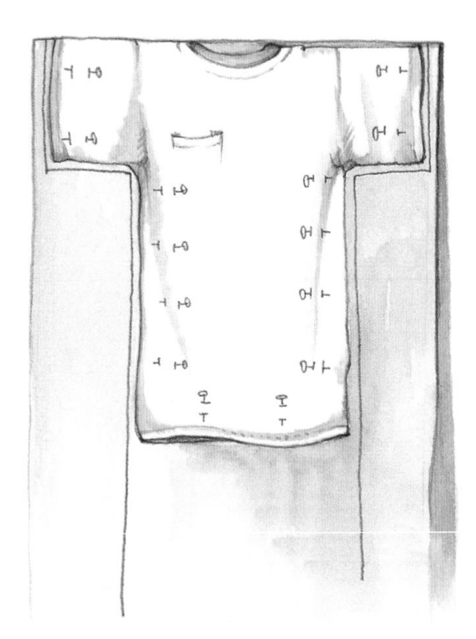

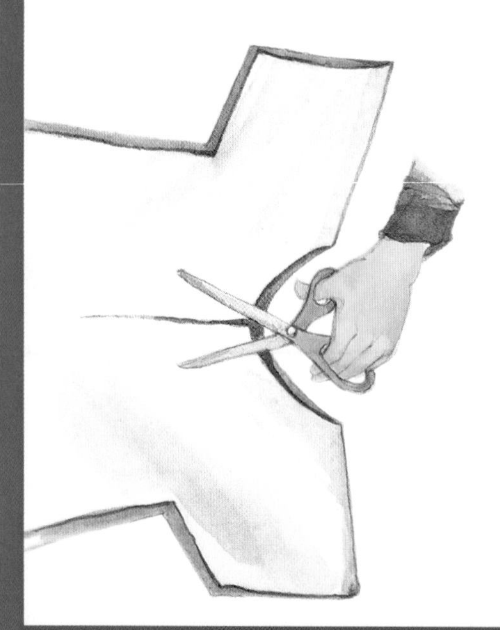

2. Cut out the neck opening. On one side of the costume, cut an 8-inch (20-centimeter) slit from the neck down the center so the costume can slip over Sadiki's head.

3. Have an adult help you pin the undersides of the sleeves and the sides of the costume together and stitch them up. Then turn the costume inside out so the stitches are hidden.

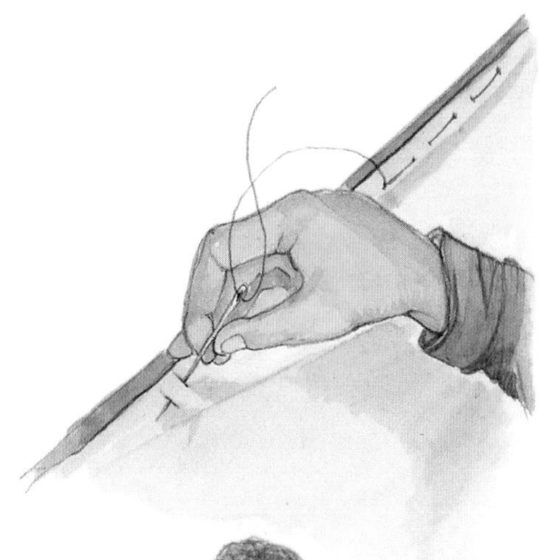

4. With markers, draw a border around the neck, cuffs, and bottom hem. Copy one or more of the African designs shown below or at the left.

Leopard, Goat, and Yam Costumes

Use paper bags for the head gear of other characters' costumes. Make the body costume the same way you made the Sadiki costume, only colored differently.

You Will Need:

large paper bags
scissors
markers
glue
yarn
cardboard
cotton balls
a small stool
a long box
a broom
tape
face paint

To Make a Leopard:

1. Cut a large hole in a bag for the actor's face.
2. Dot the bag with black or brown spots as shown.
3. Draw whiskers and a nose on your face. Glue cardboard ears to the bag.

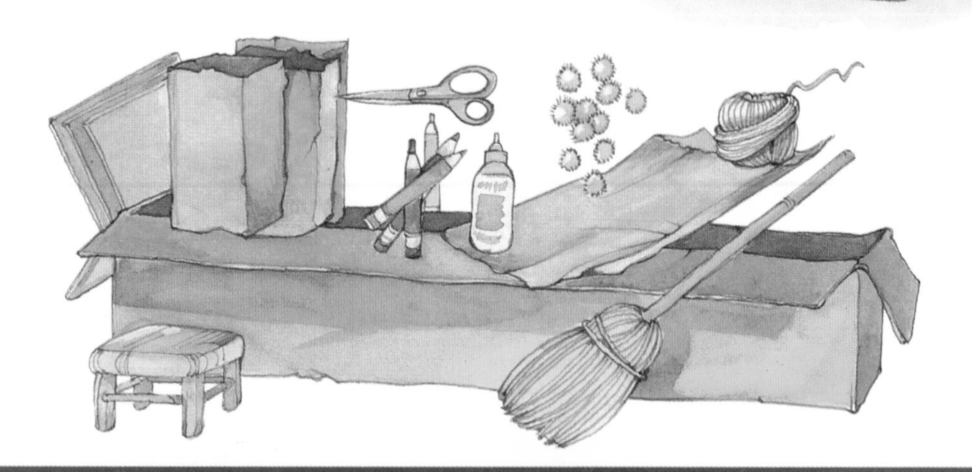

To Make a Goat:

1. Cut a large hole in a bag for the actor's face.

2. Glue cardboard ears and a goatee, or little beard, to the bag.

3. Cover the rest of the bag with cotton balls. Allow the glue to dry before using the costume.

To Make a Yam:

1. Cut a large hole in a bag for the actor's face.

2. Color the bag orange.

3. Tape leaves made of cardboard to the top.

When you look for props, use your imagination. A long, flat box can be a canoe, and a broom can be an oar. A small stool in a large paper bag would make an excellent boulder. Color the bag gray and crumple it a little.

Making Faces

A clown in baggy trousers with a big red nose runs onstage and waves to the crowd. The crowd is already giggling. Just looking at the clown's funny face makes people laugh.

Clowns use makeup to create their funny faces. Actors use makeup, too. The audience can see actors' faces more clearly when the actors wear makeup. Also, makeup can change an actor's face. For example, dark lines and white hair can make an actor look old. Green makeup can make an actor look sick or ghostly.

Some women wear makeup called cosmetics because they

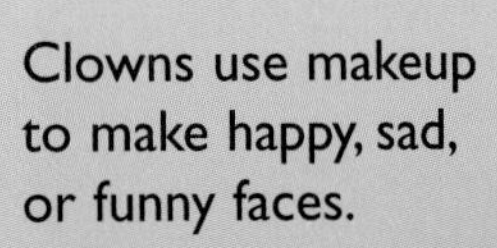

Clowns use makeup to make happy, sad, or funny faces.

Imaginative makeup turns these dancers into cats in the Broadway musical, *Cats*.

think it makes them look pretty. But clowns and actors use special makeup called grease paint. Grease paints are thick, solid sticks of colored makeup. When an actor has finished making up, he or she sprinkles the makeup with powder so that the grease paint won't smear. After the performance play, actors wipe off the grease paint with an oily makeup remover.

The Real Peter Pan

James M. Barrie

The play *Peter Pan* tells about a boy who refuses to grow up. The story sounds like make-believe. But many people believe that British playwright Sir James M. Barrie wrote the play about a real person.

Some say Barrie modeled Peter Pan after himself! Only 5 feet, 3 inches (160 centimeters) tall, Barrie always related well to children. As an 11-year-old friend told him: "You're old, but you're not grown-up. You're one of us."

Barrie said that Peter Pan was based on five boys—George, John, Peter, Michael, and Nico Davies. Barrie met their mother at a dinner party and soon became friends with her sons. Barrie told the brothers that Peter came from "the spark I got from you."

KNOW It All!

Even Nana, the Saint Bernard in *Peter Pan*, was modeled after a real dog—Barrie's pet, Porthos.

Peter Pan climbs in the window of a bedroom where he thinks he lost his shadow.

But Barrie wrote about boys who never grew up long before *Peter Pan* appeared onstage in 1904, and long before he met the Davies family. The idea may have come from his older brother.

Tall and strong, Barrie's big brother David was everything James wanted to be. But on the day before David's 14th birthday, he died in an accident. Later, James wrote: "When I became a man, [David] was still a boy of 13."

Barrie lived to be 77. Throughout his long life, he wrote fondly of people who, like David, never grew up.

Many Puppets from Many Places

What kind of performer never needs to know what he or she is going to do or say? A **puppet.** Although a puppet does not need a script, the puppeteer does. The puppeteer is the person who works the puppet.

Many puppets are hand puppets. One kind of hand puppet is called a glove

The Muppets, stars of TV and movies, are part marionette, part rod puppet.

The puppeteer puts his hand inside a mittenlike upper body to move the head and mouth. He moves the arms with a thin stick.

puppet. It has a head attached to a mittenlike upper body. The puppeteer's hand fits inside the glove. The puppeteer's thumb and fingers move the puppet's arms and head.

A **marionette** (MAR ee uh NEHT) has a whole body, including legs. Most marionettes are moved by strings that run from their head, shoulders, hands, and knees up to the control—a small wooden frame. Puppeteers hide backstage and work the marionettes by moving the controls from above.

Marionettes can make many movements, as the strings that control them are moved up and down, back and forth.

Puppeteers work rod puppets by moving rods or sticks. A rod puppet can be just a head mounted on a stick. Or it may have a complete body with movable body parts.

In Japan, rod puppets are used in a form of puppet show called *bunraku* (buhn RAH koo), or doll theater. A bunraku puppet has joints that move.

A rod puppet is a type of hand puppet. A rod is used to hold and move the puppet.

Its eyes, mouth, and even its eyebrows move, too. In other parts of Asia, rod puppets perform shadow plays. Strong lights from above and behind cast the puppets' shadows on a cloth screen. The puppets in these shadow plays are often made of leather. In China and Turkey, leather puppets are dyed, and they cast colored shadows.

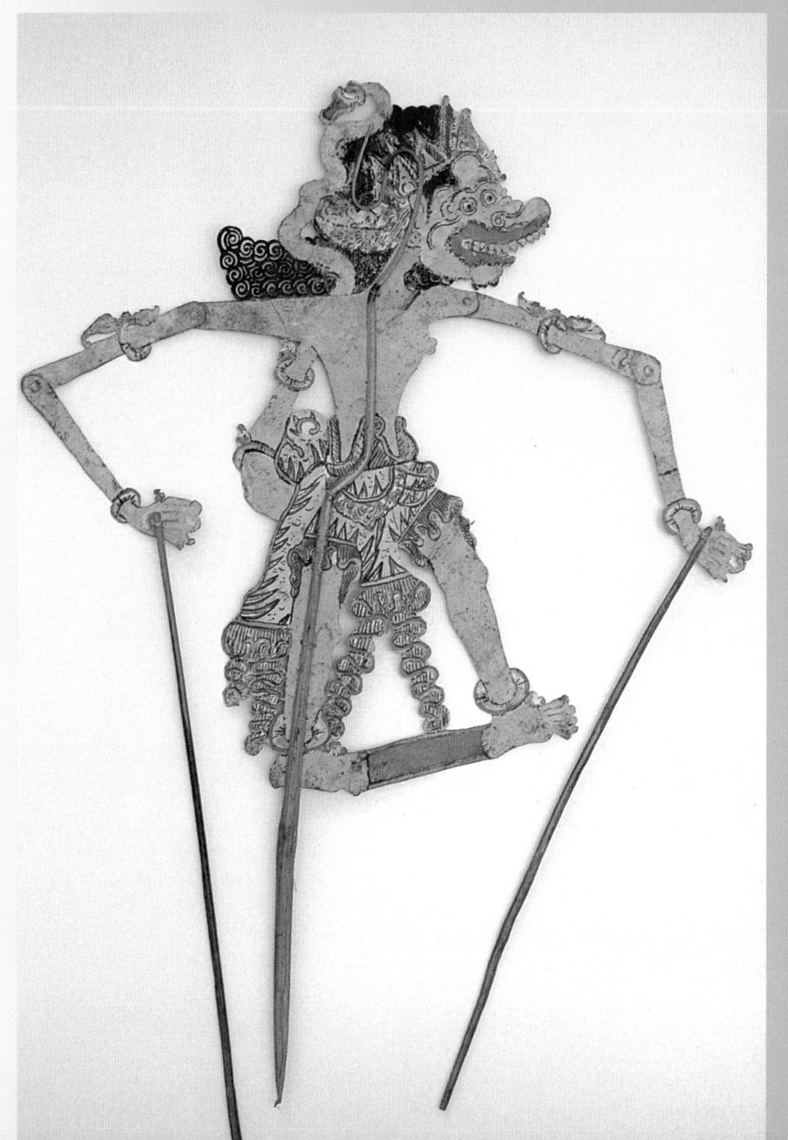

A bunraku puppet is a kind of Japanese rod puppet. It has joints that move.

Make a Glove Puppet

Putting on a puppet show is fun. But first, you have to make your cast of characters.

You Will Need:

a doll's head with a wide hole at the bottom
scissors
glue
felt, several colors
a needle
thread
a rubber band or string
straight pins

What To Do:

1. Trace the pattern at right. Cut out the tracing and pin it onto a folded piece of felt. Cut the felt around the pattern. Cut small slits as marked. Do the same with another piece of felt.

2. Sew the two pieces of felt together at the sides. Leave the neck hole open for the head. Leave the bottom open for your hand.

3. Use a head from an old plastic doll. Or buy a doll's head at a craft shop. The best heads for puppets have wide neck openings. Cover the neck on the doll's head with glue. Push the head inside the body as shown. Tie the neck hole around the neck with string or fasten it with a rubber band.

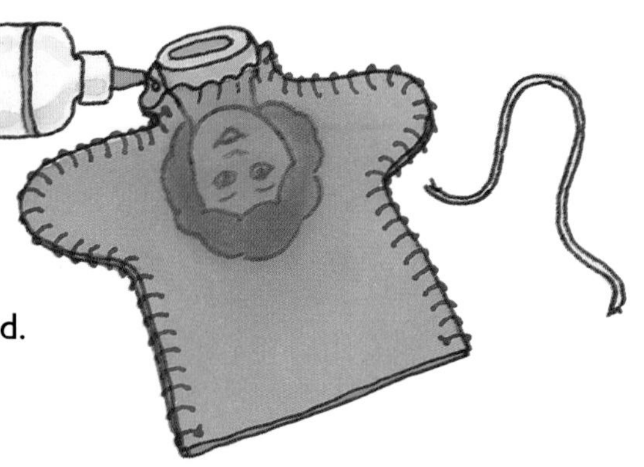

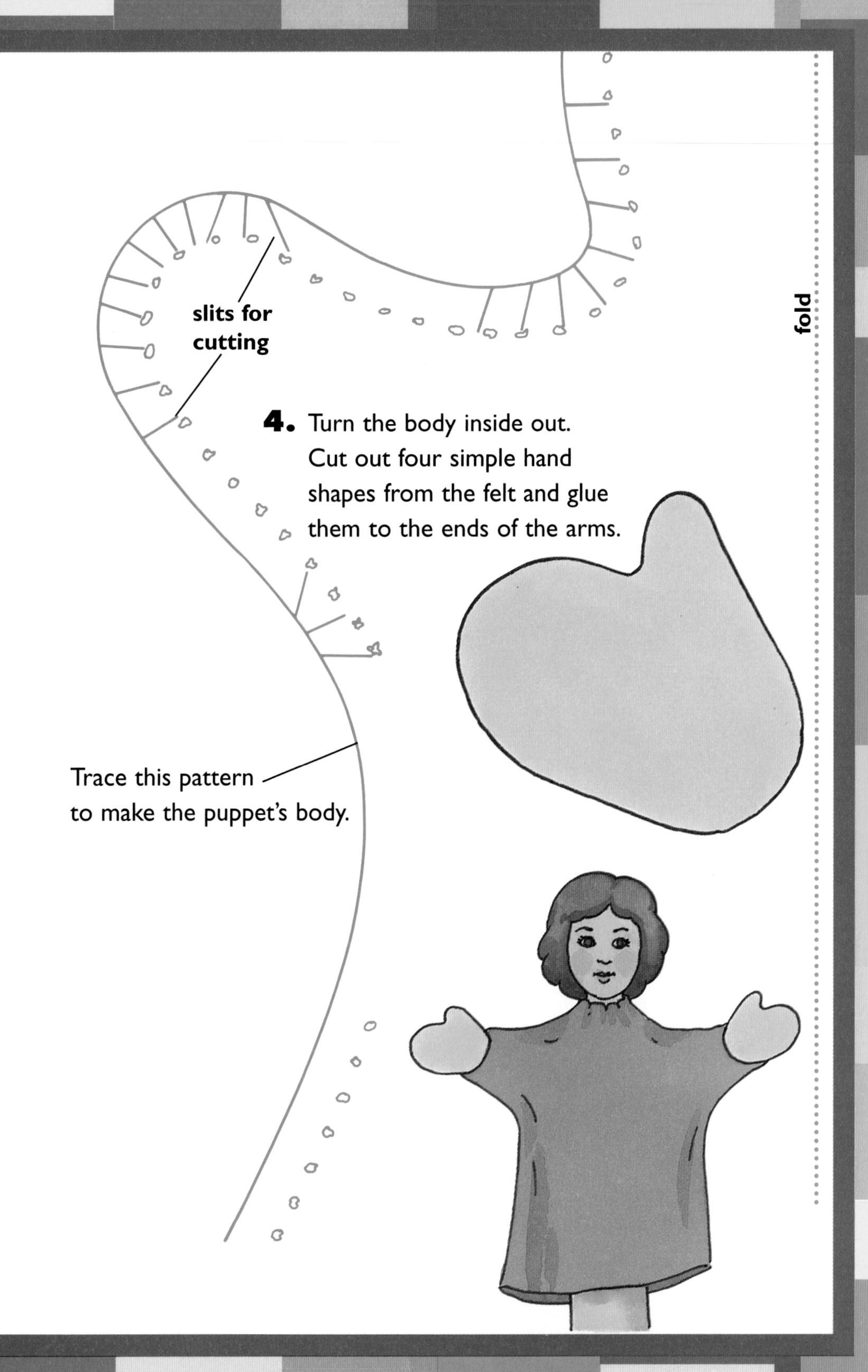

4. Turn the body inside out. Cut out four simple hand shapes from the felt and glue them to the ends of the arms.

Puppet Hats

To make your puppet one of a kind, add details, such as a crown or brimmed hat.

You Will Need:

felt
scissors
glue
straight pins
paper doilies

To Make a Crown:

1. To make a crown, cut a strip of felt long enough to go around the puppet's head and overlap a little. Cut points along the top of the strip as shown.

2. Overlap the edges and glue together. Allow the glue to dry.

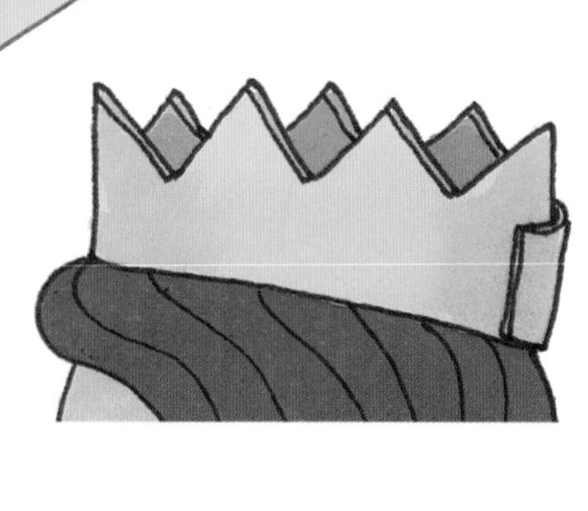

3. Add the crown and paper doilies around the neck and sleeves, and your puppet looks like a king.

To Make a Brimmed Hat:

1. To make the base of the hat, cut a strip of felt long enough to go around the puppet's head. Overlap and glue the edges.

2. To make the brim, cut a circle of felt about three times the size of the hat's base.

3. Dab glue on the bottom edge of the base. Press this edge onto the center of the brim. Wait for the glue to dry.

Stick the base or hat on the puppet's head with a straight pin.

Stage a Shadow Play

Find a coloring book that tells a story. Then turn its characters into rod puppets and create a shadow play.

You Will Need:

a coloring book
scissors
glue
cardboard
pencils
2 old sheets
masking tape
a small table
lights or floor lamps

To Make Puppets:

1. Find page-sized pictures of people and animals in the coloring book. Tear out each page. Glue each page picture-side-up on the cardboard.

2. Cut along the outline of the pictures.

3. Tape the end of a pencil to the back of each cutout.

To Make a Screen:

Ask an adult to tape an old sheet over a doorway. Place the card table behind the screen, and drape the second sheet over the table.

To Put on a Play:

1. Make up lines, or words, for each character to say. Be sure the lines tell a story.

2. Turn on lights in the room behind the screen.

3. Crouch down behind the table. Lift each puppet by the pencil on its back. Make sure that the light shines behind the puppet and casts its shadow on the screen. Remember to change your voice for each puppet when you say its lines!

Acting Without Words

Could you put on a play without saying a word? It might seem impossible. But actors have been performing plays without words for hundreds of years. Acting without speaking is called **mime**.

Actors who mime a story must use their actions to make it clear who they are, how they feel, and what they are doing. Mimes have no scenery or words

What do you think the mime in this picture is doing?

This clown is made up to look unhappy.

to help them. They show what is happening by moving their body and making faces.

Clowns also perform without speaking. But unlike mimes, clowns get help from props. For example, one clown may throw a pie at another clown to show anger. Another may dump water over his own head to make people laugh.

Clowns also use makeup to show who they are and how they feel. No two clowns paint their face in exactly the same way. Some have big smiles painted on. Others look sad and foolish—as if disaster is just around the corner.

Moving to the Music

For as long as there has been a beat there has been dance. Dance is one of the oldest forms of art. People dance to express themselves, for religious reasons, to celebrate their culture, to be with other people, for exercise, or just to have fun!

Religious dances are forms of prayer. Native Americans may dance to ask for help in hunting, farming, or war. They may imitate animals by moving like them or wearing masks. Folk dance celebrates a group's history and traditions. Folk dancers may wear colorful costumes. Many folk dances are easy to learn. People may join hands or move in a circle. Other folk dances are full of energy and passion and the dancers must be very athletic.

Some Native American dancers move and wear masks to look like certain animals.

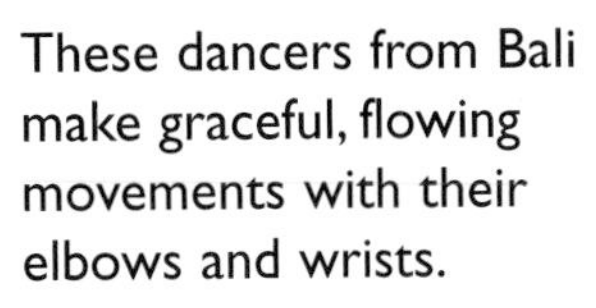

These dancers from Bali make graceful, flowing movements with their elbows and wrists.

Dancers from India swirl in a traditional dance.

We may go to a theater to see dancers who have been specially trained to perform a kind of dance. **Ballet** is the oldest kind of dance performed in theaters. It began in the 1400's at the courts of princes, dukes, and other rulers in what is now Italy. For hundreds of years, ballet dancers have made beautiful movements as they leap and twirl across the stage. Female ballet dancers, called **ballerinas,** dance on the tips of their toes

These ballet dancers are performing in *The Nutcracker.*

in special shoes. Ballet movements are very difficult. But when they are done well, they look graceful and easy.

In the late 1800's, some dancers thought that the movements in ballet were too unnatural. One of these rebels was an American dancer named Isadora Duncan. Instead of ballet steps, she made natural movements that imitated the wind and the waves. Her ideas inspired a new art form—modern dance. Several American women, including Martha Graham, continued Duncan's work. Today, even ballet dancers borrow ideas from modern dance.

Gregory Hines is a popular American tap dancer.

Another dance developed by Americans is tap. More than 100 years ago African Americans combined steps from African dances, the Irish jig, and a

Isadora Duncan rebelled against classical ballet. She was interested in personal expression and natural movement in dance.

British dance called the clog. The first "theaters" for tap dancers were taverns and street corners. But by 1870, the dancers were tapping onstage.

The musical is another mostly American form of theater dance. It tells a story through songs and dance. The dancing may have a beat, like tap, or it may move like ballet. The American movie *Singin' in the Rain*, for instance, features dancing that combines parts of ballet, jazz, modern, and tap.

Learn a Folk Dance from India

You Will Need:
- a partner
- comfortable shoes
- music from India, or your favorite tape or CD

Like folk songs, folk dances are performed by ordinary people. All people, from farmers to city workers, enjoy moving to the beat of their favorite music. Every country has certain dances that belong to its people. Asian Indians have hundreds of folk dances. Why? There are many different cultures, or groups of people, in India.

The Hikat is a dance popular with one group of people in India. This dance is a version of a children's game. Grab a partner and try out these steps.

What To Do:

1. Stretch your arms toward your partner and grip his or her wrists.

2. Lean back.

3. Turn around and around on the balls of your feet. As you spin around together, try to stay in the same circle with your feet.

4. After you try this spinning a few times, turn on the music and try to move to the beat.

Sometimes many people form a circle and clap hands. One by one, girls step into the circle and dance the Hikat in the circle's center.

Glossary

Here are some of the words you read in this book. Many of them may be new to you. Some are hard to pronounce. But since you will see them again, they are good words to know. Next to each word, you will see how to say it correctly: **ballerina** (BAL uh REE nuh). The part shown in small capital letters is said a little more loudly than the rest of the word. The part in large capital letters is said the loudest. Under each word are one or two sentences that tell what the word means.

A

assemblage (uh SEHM blihj)
An assemblage is a work of art made from scraps, junk, or odds and ends.

B

ballerina (BAL uh REE nuh)
A ballerina is a leading female ballet dancer.

ballet (bal LAY)
Ballet is a form of dance that combines traditional poses and steps with leaps and turns.

batik (buh TEEK)
Batik is an Indonesian method of printing fabric by painting parts with wax and then dyeing the fabric.

brass (bras)
Brass is a family of musical instruments. It includes such metal instruments as trumpets and trombones.

C

collage (kuh LAHZH)
A collage is a picture made up of different materials glued on a surface.

composer (kuhm POH zuhr)
A composer is a person who writes music.

contrast (KAHN trast)
Contrast is the difference between the light and dark parts of a picture.

E

embroidery (ehm BROY duhr ee)
Embroidery is the art of making decorations with needlework.

G

gamelan (GUHM uh lahn)
A gamelan is an Indonesian orchestra made up mostly of percussion instruments.

H

harmony (HAHR muh nee)
Harmony is a combination of musical notes or instruments played at the same time.

I

instrument (IHN struh muhnt)
An instrument is an object used to make music.

M

marimba (muh RIHM buh)
A marimba is a xylophone of southern Africa and Latin America with parts beneath each bar that vibrate and make the sound louder.

marionette (MAR ee uh NEHT)
A marionette is a puppet with jointed arms and legs that are moved with strings or wires.

melody (MEHL uh dee)
Melody is a rhythmic series of notes, or tune.

mime (mym)
To mime is to act a part without using words.

opera (AHP uh ruh)
An opera is a kind of play in which all or most of the lines are sung rather than spoken.

orchestra (AWR kuh struh)
An orchestra is a large group of musicians, especially including string players.

origami (AWR uh GAH mee)
Origami is the Asian craft of paper folding.

P

panpipe (PAN pyp)
A panpipe is a wind instrument made up of a series of pipes of different lengths.

papier-mâché (PAY puhr muh SHAY)
Papier-mâché is a light, strong molding material made of paper pulp and glue.

percussion (puhr KUHSH uhn)
Percussion is a family of musical instruments that make music when struck, such as drums.

perspective (puhr SPEHK tihv)
In drawing or painting, perspective is the way of showing depth and distance on a flat surface.

piñata (pee NYAH tuh)
A piñata is a decoration filled with candy and other treats, used especially in Latin American festivities.

primary colors (PRY mehr ee KUHL uhrz)
The primary colors are red, yellow, and blue. They can be mixed to make all other colors.

puppet (PUHP iht)
A puppet is a doll-like figure moved by a person called a puppeteer.

Q

quilt (kwihlt)
A quilt is a bed covering of two layers of cloth filled with padding and held together with stitching.

R

rhythm (RIHTH uhm)
Rhythm is a regular beat or accent in music.

S

secondary color (SEHK uhn dehr ee KUHL uhr)
A secondary color is purple, green, or orange. It is formed by combining two primary colors in equal parts.

silhouette (SIHL u EHT)
A silhouette is a dark shape in front of a light.

strings (strihngs)
Strings are a family of instruments that make music by vibrating strings. Violins and guitars are string instruments.

symphony (SIHM fuh nee)
A symphony is a long piece of music played by an orchestra.

synthesizer (SIHN thuh SY zuhr)
A synthesizer is a computerized electronic instrument used to produce and control sound.

T

terra cotta (TEHR uh KAHT uh)
Terra cotta is a hard, brownish-red clay.

theater (THEE uh tuhr)
Theater is a type of entertainment that includes plays and other stage performances. A theater is also the building in which such performances take place.

timpani (TIHM puh nee)
Timpani is a set of two or more drums played by one performer.

tone (tohn)
Tone is a sound with a definite pitch.

V

violin (VY uh LIHN)
A violin is a kind of stringed instrument played with a bow.

vocal cords (VOH kuhl kawrds)
Vocal cords are two small, stretchy bands in the throat that make the sound of your voice.

W

warp (wawrp)
In weaving, a warp is a series of yarns extended lengthwise in a loom and crossed by the weft.

weft (wehft)
In weaving, a weft is a filling thread or yarn.

woodwinds (WUD wihnds)
Woodwinds are a family of tubelike wood and metal instruments, such as flutes and oboes. Woodwind instruments make sounds when you blow into them.

Index

This index is an alphabetical list of important topics covered in this book. It will help you find information given in both words and pictures. To help you understand what an entry means, there is sometimes a helping word in parentheses, for example, **Aborigines** (people). If there is information in both words and pictures, you will see the words *with pictures* in parentheses after the page number. If there is only a picture, you will see the word *picture* in parentheses after the page number.

Illustration Acknowledgments

The Publishers of *Childcraft* gratefully acknowledge the courtesy of the following illustrators, photographers, agencies, and organizations for illustrations in this volume. When all the illustrations for a sequence of pages are from a single source, the inclusive page numbers are given. Credits should be read from top to bottom, left to right, on their respective pages. All illustrations are the exclusive property of the publishers of *Childcraft* unless names are marked with an asterisk (*).

Cover	Chagall mosaic—Detail from the *Four Seasons* (ca. 1974) by Marc Chagall, Bank One Plaza, Chicago © 2000 Artists Rights Society (ARS) NY/ADAGP, (photo by Cathy Melloan*); Totem—© Nancy Simmerman, Tony Stone Images*; Marionettes from Nepal—© Cathy Melloan*; African American girl painting—© Bill Losh, FPG*
Back Cover	© Nancy Simmerman, Tony Stone Images*
1	© Nancy Simmerman, Tony Stone Images*; © Cathy Melloan*; © Bill Losh, FPG*
2-3	Yoshi Miyake; © Nancy Simmerman, Tony Stone Images*; Eileen Mueller Neill
4-5	CHILDCRAFT photo by Steve Hale; Eileen Mueller Neill
6-7	Michael Charlton; Marlene Ekman; Yoshi Miyake
8-9	CHILDCRAFT photo by Allan Landau; Lisa Cinelli
10-11	Richard Hook; Lydia Halverson
12-13	Lynne Cherry; Lynne Cherry; CHILDCRAFT photo by Marshall Berman
14-15	WORLD BOOK photo by Dan Miller; © Kitz Richert*; © Kitz Richert*; © Kitz Richert*;
16-17	Robert Masheris; Robert Masheris; CHILDCRAFT photo by Russell Phillips
18-19	© Penguin Putnam, Inc.*; © S. Petegorsky Penguin Inc.*; © Penguin Putnam, Inc.*
20-21	© Montaine, Monkmeyer*; Barbara Lazarus Metz; Product Illustration, Inc.; Product Illustration, Inc.
22-23	Robert Masheris
24-25	Michael Hampshire
26-27	© Grace Welty*; Acrylic on canvas w/fabric border (1986); High Museum of Art, Atlanta, GA*
28-29	Lisa Cinelli
30-31	Robert Masheris; Robert Masheris; CHILDCRAFT photo by Russell Phillips
32-33	Silvia Balzaretti; Silvia Balzaretti; CHILDCRAFT photo by Joseph A. Erhardt
34-35	CHILDCRAFT photo by Allan Landau; Eileen Mueller Neill
36-37	Product Illustration, Inc.; WORLD BOOK photo; Product Illustration, Inc.
38-39	Eileen Mueller Neill
40-41	Jacqueline Rogers; © AAA Collection Ltd.*
42-43	Jenny Mumford
44-45	Eileen Mueller Neill
46-47	Don Simpson; Lisa Cinelli
48-49	Oil on canvas (1873) Musée D'Orsay, Paris © photo RMH (Hervé Lewandowski)*; Tim Monk
50-51	Don Simpson
52-53	International Council for Women in the Arts, Lafayette, CA*; Mixed media on handmade paper (1997) International Council for Women in the Arts, Lafayette, CA*
54-55	Oil on canvas (1885) Art Institute of Chicago, Bequest of Estelle McCormick*; © Darrell Gulin, Tony Stone Images*
56-57	Oil on canvas (1923) Art Institute of Chicago, Joseph Winterbotham Collection, 1937.188*; Oil on canvas Folkvang Museum, Essen, Germany (Superstock)*
58-59	John Lobban; Oil on canvas, (Christie's Images from Superstock)*; John Lobban
60-61	National Portrait Gallery, Smithsonian Institution (Art Resource)*; Oil on canvas (National Gallery of Art, Washington, DC (Superstock)*
62-63	Trina Schart Hyman; CHILDCRAFT photo by Russell Phillips
64-65	Ellen Raskin; Ethel Gold
66-67	Oil on canvas (late 1600's) Follower of Nicholas Poussin, National Gallery of Art, Washington, DC, Samuel H. Kress Collection; Oil on canvas Hermitage Museum, St. Petersburg, Russia (SCALA/Art Resource)*
68-69	Oil on canvas (1884) The National Gallery, London*; Eileen Mueller Neill; CHILDCRAFT photo by Russell Phillips
70-71	Hulton Getty/Liaison Agency*; Frederick Warne, Ltd. (Newberry Library, Chicago)*; Frederick Warne, Ltd. (Newberry Library, Chicago)*
72-73	Frederick Warne, Ltd. (Newberry Library, Chicago)*; Beatrix Potter*
74-75	© Christie's Images*; CHILDCRAFT photo by Russell Phillips
76-77	CHILDCRAFT photo by Russell Phillips
78-79	CHILDCRAFT photo by Joseph A. Erhardt; Lisa Cinelli
80-81	© The Bridgeman Art Library*
82-83	© Dennis Cox, ChinaStock*
84-85	Eileen Mueller Neill; CHILDCRAFT photo by Joseph A. Erhardt
86-87	Steven Brayfield
88-89	Silvia Balzaretti; Trina Schart Hyman; Silvia Balzaretti; CHILDCRAFT photo by Joseph A. Erhardt
90-91	© Robert Harding Picture Library*
92-93	Tomb of Julius II, St. Peter's Basilica, Rome (SCALA/ Art Resource)*; Marlene Ekman; Duomo, Florence, Italy (SCALA/Art Resource)*
94-95	Jean Cassels; Marlene Ekman; © Nancy Simmerman, Tony Stone Images*
96-97	© Fiona Pragoff*; © Steve Vidler, Nawrocki Stock Photo*
98-99	Private Collection (The Bridgeman Art Library)*
100-101	Marion Goodman Gallery, New York*; CHILD-CRAFT Photo by Russell Phillips
102-103	Lisa Cinelli; Linda Gist; Lisa Cinelli
104-105	Collection Kharbine-Tapabor, Paris (The Bridgeman Art Library)*; © Y. Forestier, Sygma*
106-107	© Graham Harris, Tony Stone Images*
108-109	AP/Wide World*; Yoshi Miyake
110-111	© Superstock*

112-113 Robert Byrd; © Jack Vartoogian*; Deirdre Wrobelwski
114-115 Yoshi Miyake; CHILDCRAFT photo by Steve Hale; Yoshi Miyake; Yoshi Miyake
116-117 CHILDCRAFT photo by John Walmsley; © A. K. Ortengren, Lehtikuva Oy*
118-119 CHILDCRAFT photo by Steve Hale; © Toshiro Morita, Image Life*
120-121 CHILDCRAFT photo by Steve Hale; CHILDCRAFT photo by John Walmsley
122-123 CHILDCRAFT photo by Steve Hale; Don Madden
124-125 Yoshi Miyake; CHILDCRAFT photo by Steve Hale; Yoshi Miyake
126-127 Bensen Studios, CHILDCRAFT photo by Steve Hale; Yoshi Miyake; Yoshi Miyake; Lynne Cherry
128-129 Kate Salley Palmer
130-131 © Roger Viollet from Liaison Agency*; Nan Brooks
132-133 Kate Salley Palmer; Gerardo Suzan
134-135 Don Madden; Kate Salley Palmer
136-137 © Chris MiKami, CM Photography*; AP/Wide World*
138-139 Sheila Smith
140-143 Walter Schollhammer
144-145 © Jack Vartoogian*; Marlene Ekman
146-147 Paul Williams; © Dinodia, Omni-Photo Communications*
148-149 © Jack Vartoogian*; © Paolo Koch, Photo Researchers*
150-151 Lydia Halverson; © Doug Armand, Tony Stone Images*
152-153 John Everds; © Brian Shuel, Collections*;
154-161 Marlene Ekman
162-163 © Zefa Picture Library*; Michael Charlton; AP/Wide World*
164-165 Granger Collection*; Jan Palmer; Jan Palmer
166-167 Shooting Star*; © Jeremy Horner, Panos Pictures*; © Cathy Melloan*; John Sandford
168-169 © Crispin Hughes, Panos Pictures*; © David Young-Wolff, PhotoEdit*
170-171 Eileen Mueller Neill; Product Illustration Inc.; Eileen Mueller Neill
172-175 Eileen Mueller Neill
176-177 Donald Harley; © Michael Short, Robert Harding Picture Library*
178-179 © Jack Vartoogian*; © M. Krofchack, Panos Pictures; © Jack Vartoogian*
180-181 © Tri-Star Pictures, Kobal Collection*; © Fred Fehl*; © Schloss, Hulton Getty from Liaison Agency*
182-183 Nan Brooks